"What happened when Helsinki went from a quiet city to a buzzing place full of grassroots activity and entreprneurship? Architect and designer Hella Hernberg answers this question in her new book Helsinki Beyond Dreams (...), in which she champions local cultures that make a big difference."
   – MONOCLE / ELNA NYKÄNEN-ANDERSSON

"Helsinki Beyond Dreams (...) is an exceptionally illuminating journey into new urban phenomena, such as urban agriculture, neighborhood events, Restaurant Days and many other fruitful citizen initiatives."
   "The citizens of Helsinki are now freer than ever to pursue their ideas and inventions. (...) Helsinki Beyond Dreams leads the way and inspires."
   – HELSINGIN SANOMAT / PEKKA SAURI, DEPUTY MAYOR OF HELSINKI

"The 27 texts (...) are consistently relevant. They touch upon important and topical issues, they are entertaining and above all, they give the reader hope, not just for a better city but for a better world."
   – ARK (THE FINNISH ARCHITECTURAL REVIEW) / HENNU KJIISIK

"Helsinki Beyond Dreams illustrates how LQC [lighter, quicker, cheaper] interventions add up to a whole that is greater than the sum of its parts by generating a more robust public discussion around public space. For that alone – never mind the crisp writing and beautiful illustrations – the book is well worth a read."
   – PROJECT FOR PUBLIC SPACES / BRENDAN CRAIN

"An obscenely good looking book that talks about Helsinki with love."
   – NYT MAGAZINE / MATTI KOSKINEN

HELSINKI BEYOND DREAMS

© **Hella Hernberg et al**

All rights reserved. No part of this book may be used or reproduced in any manner whatsoever without written permission by the publisher and the artists, except in the case of brief quotations embodied in crtitical articles and reviews.

Editor-in-chief: Hella Hernberg

Writers:
Antti Alavuotunki, Bryan Boyer, Elissa Eriksson, Hella Hernberg, Timo Hyppönen, Paavo Järvensivu, Ilpo Kiiskinen, Heta Kuchka, Ida Kukkapuro, Tommi Laitio, Meri Louekari, Katharina Moebus, OK Do, Joel Rosenberg, Timo Santala, Tuomas Siitonen, Valtteri Väkevä

Photographers:
Charlotta Boucht, Stefan Bremer, Sebastian Greger, Katja Hagelstam, Tuomas Jääskeläinen, Tuukka Kaila, Kirmo Kivelä, Hanna Koikkalainen, Veikko Kähkönen, Carl Sebastian Lindberg, Andreas Meichsner, Johannes Romppanen, Tuomas Sarparanta, Tani Simberg, Juha Snellman, Heli Sorjonen, Matti Tanskanen, Antti Tuomola, Heidi Uutela

Illustrators:
Sac Magique, Sanna Pelliccioni, Pent Talvet, Nene Tsuboi

Art director: Timo Tuomas

English editor: James Clay

Translations:
Katarina Murto (pp. 22-27, 60-77, 102-106, 118-121, 140-151, 172-179), Lissu Moulton (pp.56-59)

Cover and chapter illustrations: Sac Magique
Map illustration: Pent Talvet

Photographs on the first and last pages:
p.2: Geese watching the view from Kalasatama harbor towards Hanasaari and Merihaka. Photo: Johannes Romppanen. p.4: Wannabe Ballerinas performing at the 2011 Punajuuri Blockparty. Photo: Carl Sebastian Lindberg. p.6: The Kallion Herkut (Delicacies of Kallio) restaurant at August 2011's Restaurant Day. Photo: Tuomas Sarparanta. p.184: The self-built skate park in Kalasatama. Photo: Johannes Romppanen.

Publisher: Urban Dream Management, Helsinki

Printed in Estonia
ISBN 978-952-93-2538-2
Second edition, 2013
First published in 2012

Orders: www.helsinkibeyonddreams.com

HELLA HERNBERG (ED.)

Helsinki Beyond Dreams

ACTIONS TOWARDS A CREATIVE
AND SUSTAINABLE HOMETOWN

URBAN DREAM MANAGEMENT

Contents

17   Foreword

19   Acknowledgements

1. Re-Imagining Helsinki

22   **The City Belongs to Us**
We Love Helsinki and positive civil disobedience
TIMO SANTALA

28   **Unfinished City**
Changing landscapes breathe with a new energy
HELLA HERNBERG, PHOTOS: CHARLOTTA BOUCHT

36   **The Battle Against Apathy**
A short history of urban activism in Helsinki
HELLA HERNBERG

42   **Hello From the Future**
Imagining the possibilities for a better city
OK DO & BRYAN BOYER, ILLUSTRATIONS: NENE TSUBOI

46   **Helsinki Internationals**
Immigrant perspectives on Helsinki
HELLA HERNBERG, PHOTOS: JOHANNES ROMPPANEN

2. Everyman's Urbanism

56 Home Street Home
The Story of Punajuuri Block Party
HETA KUCHKA, PHOTOS: TANI SIMBERG

60 The City as I Want to See It
Commenting on the city through urban art
ELISSA ERIKSSON

68 Tango Around Town
Vallilan Tango heralds a rebirth for traditional dances
ANTTI ALAVUOTUNKI & ILPO KIISKINEN
PHOTOS: HELI SORJONEN & HANNA KOIKKALAINEN

74 Tuomas is (Still) Here
Growing up with graffiti
TUOMAS SIITONEN

78 Helsinki Through a Skateboarder's Eye
Window shopping for perfect surfing spots
VALTTERI VÄKEVÄ, PHOTOS: TUUKKA KAILA

84 The City of Children
Children's visions in town planning
HELLA HERNBERG

3. Hidden Treasures

90   **Kalasatama Temporary**
The new playground for grassroots culture
HELLA HERNBERG, PHOTOS: JOHANNES ROMPPANEN

102   **A Pearl at the end of the Orange Line**
Neighborhood democracy and local affection in suburbia
TOMMI LAITIO, PHOTOS: MATTI TANSKANEN

106   **Independent Shops Make a Comeback**
A walk through the rejuvenation of an old workers' district
HELLA HERNBERG, PHOTOS: JOHANNES ROMPPANEN

114   **Literary Interventions**
The story of the first Museum of the Near Future
OK DO

118   **Opening Doors to Helsinki's Hidden Places**
Old and new jewels rediscovered via OpenHouseHelsinki
MERI LOUEKARI

4. Actions for Real Food

124   **The Quest for Bread**
Reawakening bread culture in Helsinki
KATHARINA MOEBUS

132   **Notes from an Urban Farmer**
Greening the city's empty corners
HELLA HERNBERG

140   **The Day of Independent Restaurateurs**
Restaurant Day: the DIY food carnival goes global
IDA KUKKAPURO

148   **Is It Safe to Eat These?**
Foraging and harvesting public trees and bushes in the city
JOEL ROSENBERG, PHOTOS: JOHANNES ROMPPANEN

152   **Cooking Under the Sun**
Hot dishes from the Solar Kitchen – if you're lucky
HELLA HERNBERG, PHOTOS: JOHANNES ROMPPANEN

5. Slow vs. Grow

158 A Tale of Two Hearts
Will Tallinn and Helsinki merge into a twin city?
BRYAN BOYER, ILLUSTRATION: PENT TALVET

162 Lessons from the Summer Cottage
Reinventing modest Finnish traditions
HELLA HERNBERG

168 A New Horizon
Testing manpower in the city and beyond
TIMO HYPPÖNEN

172 More than Money
Time banking and alternative economies
HELLA HERNBERG, ILLUSTRATIONS: SANNA PELLICCIONI

176 The New Life of Things
Lending is the future
HELLA HERNBERG

180 Helsinki Beyond the Economy?
Can Helsinki take a lead in fostering immaterial values?
PAAVO JÄRVENSIVU, ILLUSTRATIONS: PENT TALVET

186 Contributors

188 Sources and Inspiration

190 Map of Articles

Aerial view of central Helsinki shows the main locations under transformation: 1.Pasila, 2.Kalasatama, 3.Jätkäsaari, 4.The oil harbor. Photo courtesy of the City Survey Division, Helsinki.

The opening of the shore route at Kalasatama harbor on Helsinki Day, June 2010. The new route made the old cargo port's shoreline accessible to everyone. Photo: Hella Hernberg

Foreword

"It takes creative individuals with determination and indomitable will to propel the innovation that society needs to tackle its toughest problems."

– DAVID BORNSTEIN

Dear Reader,

You are witness to a documentary of a new Helsinki, a city where grassroots culture is flourishing. In the past few years our previously quiet and reserved Nordic hometown has been a source of constant surprise. Thanks to a new we-spirit and the enthusiasm of its people, Helsinki is breaking free and becoming a more intriguing and enjoyable place – a city where you can feel at home.

The Finnish traditions of *"sisu"* and "everyman's rights" are merging into a new urban attitude that has the potential to take Helsinki beyond our dreams. Sisu is our word for fortitude – the special Finnish kind of perseverance and guts.

This book tells the story of sisu as it is manifested in people's passion to make our city's corners better places to live. It is about small endeavors that question common conventions and contribute to the common good, building from the ground up. It is the entrepreneurial spirit of the lady who runs a container café in the middle of an empty harbor; the girl who builds a public outdoor oven in her quest for better bread; the immigrants who, regardless of language barriers, start running businesses; the grandmothers who team up to turn a disreputable park into an urban living room; or the friends who encourage people to join Restaurant Day and open up one-day restaurants in celebration of food culture.

Helsinki Beyond Dreams itself is also something of a collective grassroots activity. The book has been written, edited and photographed by a culturally varied group of urban activists, thinkers, designers and artists.

In the background this project has been driven by *Urban Dream Management,* a design practice that focuses on creative solutions for more sustainable and enjoyable urban living.

I started planning this book in fall 2010 with a hunch that there was something new bubbling under in Helsinki. I invited people to join and write about their personal views and projects.

Still, I could only have dreamed about the explosion of new urban events and initiatives that came to fruition during 2011 – just in time to be documented on these pages.

This book is part of the official program of World Design Capital Helsinki 2012. In uncovering this collection of urban tales I hope to continue to stimulate the debate on how strategic design could contribute to a better, more open city and society. Developing systems that facilitate people's ideas and dreams, rather than restraining them, is a key challenge facing our community.

As I finished compiling the first edition of this book it was New Year 2012 and Helsinki was celebrating its first days as World Design Capital. Since the launch of Helsinki Beyond Dreams in April 2012 we have seen an unimaginable number of exciting new initiatives, events and discussions.

What was written in the original introduction has already proved true: "This is certainly just a start and there will be many more inspiring ideas and fascinating people involved in the future." Restaurant Day has grown into an international festival, and has been followed by new initiatives, such as "Cleaning Day" that turns the city's parks and streets into a big flea market. Other new neighborhood movements are also rising up in Töölö, Kallio and elsewhere in the city.

Helsinki Beyond Dreams has found its way onto the desks of civil servants in municipalities and government, hopefully laying the groundwork for better dialogue between citizens, planners and decision-makers. The book has been reviewed with enthusiasm and featured in English, Finnish, German, Italian and Swedish journals and periodicals, and has been represented at events and exhibitions in Helsinki, New York, London and beyond.

Helsinki is now in the midst of several impactful urban construction and renewal projects, with decades of major transformation ahead. Our city has the potential to evolve in many different directions. We can see that the seeds of a new urban happiness are germinating, though they need tending. Our strong local culture of grassroots innovation is still an underutilized resource – but it has the potential to really make Helsinki the best place in the world.

A major discussion is underway on how new citizen initiatives could develop into more long-term processes, and how the newly discovered we-spirit could become part of our everyday lives – in the suburbs beyond central Helsinki and in smaller towns. Designers are taking the first steps to integrate with public bodies, with the aim of redesigning bureaucratic processes to meet future challenges, in dialogue with citizens.

Through these inspiring stories of creative endeavor and innovation, we hope to stir up the collective spirit – where citizens, designers, decision-makers and planners work together for more livable, enjoyable and sustainable cities – anywhere in the world.

Jätkäsaari, Helsinki
20 June 2013
Hella Hernberg

PS The content of this second edition is the same as in the original first edition, except for this updated foreword and minor corrections.

"The only limits are, as always, those of vision."
– JAMES BROUGHTON

Acknowledgements

This book wouldn't have been possible without all the people that devoted their time and energy to organizing the wonderful and inspiring events and activities that fill these pages.

I want to take the opportunity to thank all these people. Firstly for re-imagining their piece of the city, and secondly for their willingness to join and contribute to this book – either in the form of their own essays or through interviews. Their enthusiasm and positive feedback have kept our spirits high during this project.

Special thanks go to all the photographers and illustrators involved, including those that warmly welcomed us to dig into their archives, and others that faithfully documented and illuminated current events. It has been rewarding to meet so many talented professionals inspired to take part in such an independent publication. I am especially grateful to **Johannes Romppanen** and **Sac Magique** for their devotion to the project.

It was our ambition to make the book an enjoyable read in English. I want to thank our English editor, **James Clay**, for his appreciation of all things "Finnglish." Warmest thanks to **Timo Hyppönen**, for his vision and feedback, and for providing his insight and support throughout the whole project.

Helsinki's appointment as World Design Capital 2012 gave this project great momentum. I want to thank the producers of WDC Helsinki 2012, **Martta Louekari** and **Milla Visuri** in particular, for their encouragement to develop the project further from the seeds of the initial idea.

The support and faith of so many friends, family members and colleagues has been vital. I am especially thankful to **Anu-Elina Lehti, Reetta Haarajoki** and to my mother for their fruitful comments on the book's raw version. Our layout team is grateful to **Timo Kirves** for sharing his technical expertise on the secrets of graphic reproduction.

Finally, a project involving such a large group of collaborators would not have been realized without the financial support provided by the following foundations: *National Council for Architecture, Alfred Kordelin Foundation, Arts Council of Helsinki Metropolitan Region,* and *Grafia.*

There are certainly many events and endeavors that have not found their way to the pages of this book. Nonetheless all of them are important as they all contribute to the good spirit that makes our city a better place. Let's continue building even better future dreams together!

1. Re-Imagining Helsinki

In the coming decades, Helsinki will undergo massive urban change. Beyond the building sites and cranes the city is full of untapped potential. Who will the new Helsinki belong to? Why do we love our city, and how will we improve it?

The City Belongs to Us

We Love Helsinki encourages people to take over their city.

TEXT: TIMO SANTALA

If you run into a group of strangers that are playing tag in Helsinki's biggest department store, dancing the *Letkajenkka* folk dance around the clock tower in a central square, or singing group karaoke on an outdoor terrace, don't be surprised – join them! You've just met *We Love Helsinki*, a group that makes communal interventions around the city.

We Love Helsinki happenings are often unusual and surprising. A water gun fight between hundreds of people can suddenly break out on the beach. A river raft may transform into a dance floor for enraptured dance partners passionately twirling to tango.

We Love Helsinki constantly tests the limits of urban spaces and plays with the idea of "what if?".

The events don't have performers. Instead people themselves create the mood by taking part and doing things together. At We Love Helsinki events, every stranger is an opportunity – a potential friend and someone you can have fun with. During the communal street art tour people were armed with colorful contact paper, sticky tape and scissors, and turned booths, poles and electricity boxes into living creatures that had eyes, mouths, noses, hands and feet.

"We have the right – and also the duty – to use urban spaces and to take responsibility for them."

But what is We Love Helsinki really about? Most of all, it's an attitude.

The city is ours and it must be loved. Home is not something confined within four walls but it extends across the entire city. We have the right – and also the duty – to use urban spaces and to take responsibility for them. The city isn't a mere static structure made up solely of physical attributes. It is a living and

Above: During the 2011 We Love Helsinki festival a cable ferry on the Aura river in Turku became a passionate platform for tango. Maija Juutilainen and Tuuli Hongisto dance away the summer evening (Photo: Tuomas Sarparanta).
Below: City rides have united Helsinki cyclists in calls for improved cycle lanes (Photo: Timo Santala).

Reijo Aittakumpu conducting the 2000-strong choir at the 2011 "Choir Corridor." Listeners could walk along the choir and hop in to sing along to the custom composed Helsinki Anthem (Photo: Timo Santala).

A huge water gun fight has become a tradition of the We Love Helsinki festival (Photo: Timo Santala). The communal "Street Art Tour" in 2011 transformed poles and booths into living creatures (Photo: Tuomas Sarparanta). The "Block Full of Sound" event invited anyone to play – Pintandwefall were among the independent bands and amateur street musicians on show (Photo: Timo Santala). At the 2010 "Art Battle" graffiti and other artists painted live, and the winner invited kids from the audience to paint (Photo: Antti ˉuomola).

At We Love Helsinki's traditional dances, classic waltzes, tangos, foxtrots and hits from the 1930-70's inspire modern young urbanites to put on their flowery dresses and gentlemen's hats (Photo: Timo Santala).

organic entity. A city is formed through actions and its atmosphere is created by people and their encounters. The city is an open space that residents should appropriate and cultivate as they see fit – instead of waiting for established institutions to do it for them. Streets, parks and squares should be taken over and fashioned into urban living rooms, into spaces where people can interact and really get together.

Urban culture is undergoing transformation. People want to be involved and do things themselves instead of passively consuming cultural offerings handed down from distant organizations. This idea is at the heart of We Love Helsinki.

This "what if" thinking has also led to Restaurant Day (see p.140), an event where anyone can set up a restaurant for a day. This is exactly the kind of positive civil disobedience that we need in order to encourage people to spread their wings and realize their dreams.

> "A city is formed through actions and its atmosphere is created by the people and their encounters."

Right now Helsinki is bubbling with events organized by the people. The city is raising a generation that think that it's completely normal and natural to set up a restaurant in a park, to start a garden on a roof top, or to close a street to traffic for a block party.

By doing things together we lay the foundations for the civil society of the future – a society based on active citizenship, the common good and caring for other people. ■

The 2010 We Love Helsinki Festival kicked off with public declarations of love for Helsinki. People drew their fondest memories of the city on the asphalt. At the same time there was a cheerful world-record attempt for the longest "letkajenkka" folk dance line (Photo: Timo Santala).

Unfinished City

The changing landscapes of Helsinki are breathing new energy into the city. Empty harbors and unused buildings are acting as catalysts for new ideas and events. But are bottom-up initiatives and their potential akcnowledged officially as a resource for urban development?

TEXT: HELLA HERNBERG · PHOTOS: CHARLOTTA BOUCHT

A photo from 1907 by **Signe Brander** shows laundry drying on tree branches in a park that no longer exists in what is now downtown Helsinki. Brander documented changing city scenes in Helsinki a century ago. Her images showed wooden houses and fishermen's huts as they were about to disappear under the developing metropolis.

During the last 100 years, Helsinki has grown dramatically and whole new districts have been born. At the beginning of the 20th century, many of our inner-city neighborhoods, such as *Töölö, Haaga, Käpylä and Pasila*, were only meadows and barely existed as sketches. While the Civil War raged in 1918, architects like **Eliel Saarinen** made wild plans for Helsinki's future growth.[1]

Helsinki is a comparatively young city without as many historical layers as the medieval cities of central Europe, not to mention ancient cities, such as Rome. Founded at the mouth of the river Vantaa in 1550, Helsinki remained little more than a hamlet for centuries, before the first parts of its current center were built about six kilometers to the south on the Helsinki Peninsula in the early 19th century. In 1809 Finland became part of Russia and in 1812 Helsinki was appointed the new capital of the autonomous Grand Duchy of Finland.

"The incredible scale and breadth of Helsinki's development has created a new vitality."

Laundry drying in the Tehtaanpuisto park, Eira, 1907. Photo by Signe Brander / Photo courtesy of Helsinki City Museum.

Restructuring Helsinki

In 2012 we are living on the verge of a great urban renovation. Helsinki will continue to expand faster than ever before within the coming decades. With 577,000 inhabitants in 2011, the population is estimated to grow by 10% by the year 2030.

Grand new city districts will be built close to the existing city center, along with the expansion of a number of older neighborhoods. The redevelopment of the city will create over seven million square meters of new domestic and commercial floor space in eleven distinct development zones.²

Infrastructural changes have made large areas available for new developments within the inner city. In 2008 two of Helsinki's central cargo ports were relocated to the outlying eastern suburb of *Vuosaari*. The oil terminal in eastern Helsinki has also been cleared for a new residential district called *Kruunuvuorenranta*, the construction of which is about to begin in 2012.

Helsinki's development situation is unique. How many other established capital cities have such vast spatial reserves in close proximity to the city center?

The harbors, shipyards and railway tunnels of these former industrial areas used to be relatively hidden, inaccessible parts of the city. Their industrial feel is a refreshing contrast to Helsinki's residential and commercial landscape. During the unique time these spaces await major construction, their undefined and temporary nature is an inspiring feature of a new Helsinki.

This is the time to take your bike and explore the areas waiting for change: the rail yards in Pasila and *Vallila*, the abandoned villas next to the old oil harbor, the old central railway tunnel connecting Töölö Bay to *Ruoholahti*, the shipyards of *Hernesaari*, and the tarmac wilderness of *Kalasatama* harbor.

Portraits of Change

Photographer **Charlotta Boucht** is one of those who have been fascinated by changing city scenes in Helsinki. She has been documenting the recent removal of cylindrical storage tanks from the oil harbor. The sight of the oil depot looming on the horizon is familiar to Helsinkians but few of us have had permission to visit the site.

"The harbors, shipyards and railway tunnels of these former industrial areas used to be relatively hidden, inaccessible parts of the city. Their undefined and temporary nature is an inspiring feature of a new Helsinki."

Boucht has been thrilled by the oil harbor: "The round containers standing on a hill create such a stunning atmosphere, like a small city of its own. It has been a great privilege to document this strange but beautiful disappearing scenery. In the autumn the place was almost magical – desolate and silent – with the hum of machines in the background. From Kruunuvuorenranta, fantastic views open up to the city centre. Even though I understand the new residential area will be needed, it breaks my heart to think I can't come back to greet these big 'cans' anymore."

It is not only artists that see the beauty in industry. Boucht recalls when she photographed the large coal mountains serving the energy plant in uptown Helsinki. "I went to a worker man asking, 'isn't this so beautiful?' and, to my great surprise, he got almost poetic, describing in many words how sometimes the small bits of coal start burning by themselves and how you can see small flames and sparks in the air."

Thinking back to Signe Brander's times, in the context of Helsinki's current upheaval, perhaps a hundred years doesn't seem such a long time. What will happen in the next few decades is somewhat more difficult to grasp. The new districts planned to be built around *Jätkäsaari*, Kalasatama, Kruunuvuorenranta and other areas, will form a significant portion of the future City of Helsinki. The contributors to this book might be retired by the time these areas are finalized. What will the city look like to their grandchildren?

New Energy for New Ideas

The incredible scale and breadth of Helsinki's development has created a new vitality. Areas under transformation serve as catalysts for new things and ideas. Open playgrounds, such as Kalasatama, have become new stages for civic grassroots activities and derelict warehouses have become home to startup businesses, art projects and creative networks.

Architect, D.Sc **Panu Lehtovuori** has done extensive research on temporary uses of those spaces lying in wait for the future.[3] He points out that temporary uses are an underutilized resource of urban planning. In a recent proposal, *Kaupunkikiihdytin* (Urban Accelerator),[4] carried out by *Livady Architects* in collaboration with the Ministry of the Environment, Lehtovuori suggests that temporary uses should be taken

Re-Imagining Helsinki 31

The cylindrical oil storage tanks at Helsinki's oil harbor in 2010, before their removal.

The Kalasatama harbor area waiting for new construction work to start in 2010, after the cargo port had been demolished and transported to the eastern district of Vuosaari.

seriously and placed at the very nucleus of urban politics and planning. "New radical culture, such as experimental theater or new music, flourishes in temporary spaces. They are part of the pluralistic culture of big metropolises. Authentic cultural actors or startup businesses are crucial to cities' success in global competition. Temporary, experimental projects act as 'place-makers,' turning as yet undefined locations into something unique with a new, distinct identity – while helping introducing the areas to the public. They may also be profitable for real estate owners, increasing property value through a new image. Even cheap rents can cover the maintenance costs of buildings lying unused."

> "Independent cafés, teashops, galleries, bakeries and organic food shops are springing up – the kind you wouldn't have found here only a few years ago. These new cottage industries are to be applauded."

Despite the potential, good ideas often tend to get stuck in bureaucracy, and many great locations are left unused. Lehtovuori explains that there is a strong need for specific legislation regarding temporary use of space. For example, certain building regulations and permits could be stretched a little.

"Regarding the permissions and procedures allowing temporary use, cultural values should also be understood and seen as a valid argument next to the narrow real-estate business perspective."

In the Urban Accelerator model, Lehtovuori suggests that a mediator specialized in temporary uses would be needed: a professional who understands the needs of both real estate owners and the potential temporary users. For example, in the Netherlands this model has been successfully tested. One case is the re-use of the NDSM shipyard in Amsterdam. This formerly remote area has developed into an attractive spot through temporary cultural use.

In Finland, a new company called *Hukkatila* (Leftover space) was founded in fall 2011 after winning the *Peloton* idea competition for energy-efficient projects. The company aims to tap into the resource of unused spaces throughout Finland and mediate them to the right users.

Grassroots Innovation as a Resource

Recent examples of citizen activism and social innovation show that there is a new surge of energy in Helsinki that was not present before. People throw block parties in the street, adopt empty lots for gardening, and organize night bicycle rides – just to celebrate the beauty of the city. Compare this new dynamic with the 1970's when it would have been inconceivable to see someone playing guitar in front of Helsinki's railway station without police intervention. It is as if people have rediscovered what we Finns call our everyman's rights – a legal concept that we can now apply to our new relationship with the urban environment.

In addition to what's going on in vacant harbor areas, attractive outlets are rapidly filling the streets of the city centre. Independent cafés, teashops, galleries, bakeries and organic food shops are springing up – the kind you wouldn't have found here only a few years ago. These new cottage industries are to be applauded. For those dreaming of selling food or alcohol in Helsinki, it takes perseverance to claw your way through the jungle of safety regulations, while competing against the major chains that dominate Finnish grocery retail.

The view from Hietalahti dockyard towards Jätkäsaari harbor in 2010.

Helsinki will grow at incredible speed in the next few decades and many unknowns lay ahead. Citizens' own self-generated projects demonstrate that great transformative power lies in people themselves. Now that many grand urban projects are about to get started, a key question is how to integrate creative citizen initiatives with the long term planning process? Planning does matter, but it only offers a framework.

As Helsinki celebrates World Design Capital 2012, a question arises: how can design assist in building a better dialogue between bottom-up activities and top-down decision-making? Design is already moving further from its traditional area towards "design thinking," which addresses methods and processes rather than products. Designing new systems for a better functioning society that can utilize its potential both on an official and a spontaneous

The Pasila rail yard, looking towards West Pasila.

level is a key area for development. The best results are achieved when decision-making and citizens' ideas are allowed to interact and grow together in symbiosis.

---

1 Jung, Bertel; Saarinen, Eliel (1918). *Ett förslag till stadsplan för "Stor Helsingfors": Pro Helsingfors*. Helsinki: Lilius & Hertzberg
Hietala Marjatta; Helminen Martti; Lahtinen Merja (2009). *Helsinki - Historic Town Atlas*. City of Helsinki Statistical Office.

2 http://en.uuttahelsinkia.fi/sections/2/overview (20.12.2011)

3 See, for example: the "Urban Catalyst" research project.
Lehtovuori, Panu; Hentilä, Helka-Liisa; Bengs, Christer (2003). *Temporary uses. The Forgotten Resource of Urban Planning. Urban Catalysts*. Helsinki University of Technology, Centre for Urban and Regional Studies, Series C.

Lehtovuori, Panu (2005). *Experience and Conflict: the dialectics of the production of urban space in the light of new venues in Helsinki 1993-2003*. Doctoral thesis, Helsinki University of Technology, Centre for Urban and Regional Studies, Espoo.

4 Lehtovuori, Panu; Ruoppila, Sampo (2011). *Kaupunkikiihdytin - Tilapäiset käytöt kehittämisen voimavarana*. Helsinki: Livady Architects / Ministry of the Environment.
http://www.livady.fi/303/kaupunkikiihdytin_pieni.pdf

The Battle Against Apathy

30 years ago Helsinki was perceived as a culturally barren enclave of the Eastern Bloc. The riotous underground venue Lepakko, the transformation of the old cable factory, and the rejuvenation of power plants and railway buildings, have all contributed to a cultural renaissance that has laid the foundations for today's citizen-led grassroots actions.

TEXT: HELLA HERNBERG

Before 9 am on Sunday 19 August 1979, a group of activists led by a 22-year-old **Teemu Lehto** were walking towards an old warehouse at the junction of the *Länsiväylä* highway, which leads west from Helsinki. Originally built as a paint factory, the warehouse had worked as a shelter for homeless alcoholics for the previous 12 years, and had been empty since midsummer. The shelter had been nicknamed *Liekkihotelli* (Flame Hotel) after the guests' favorite drink of household cleaning liquid – denatured ethanol with a flame on the bottle's label.

Armed with nothing more than cleaning utensils, Lehto and about 20 other youngsters prepared to take over the building and turn it into a house of music. War veteran **Aaro Syvänen**, a frequent guest of the former shelter, still lived there and had left a few windows open, so their task was easy. Lehto climbed in through the window and opened the doors for the cleaning crew.

A new page was turned in the history of urban culture in Helsinki. After some relatively lightweight arm wrestling with Helsinki city's leaders, the old warehouse became a legendary arena for music and for all kinds of alternative culture for the following twenty years, led by the newly founded live music association, *Elmu*.[1]

Lepakkoluola (the Bat Cave), or simply *Lepakko*, became a living legend. One story

The Bat Cave is taken over. Photo: Valtter Schubin, 1979.

The Lepakko building in 1991. Photo: Jan Alaco / Photo courtesy of Helsinki City Museum.

tells of how the new name came about from the old paint factory's logo, from a butterfly that, in some people's eyes, looked more like a bat.

As one of the murals on the Bat Cave's walls declared, a "war against apathy" had begun in this legendary Helsinki squat. The Elmu live music association had been founded in 1978 to serve a real need. There simply wasn't live music in Helsinki.

Teemu Lehto, today a time researcher and IT consultant, recalls: "Helsinki was totally dead in the 1970's. The only live music venues were the *Tavastia* club – still running since 1970 – and a few student union places. The 30% 'amusement tax' made certain that performing live remained unprofitable. There were lots of enthusiastic bands and audiences, but simply no places to meet, so Elmu was born."

From the perspective of 2012, the Helsinki of the 1970's seems a world away. Finland, at the armpit of the Soviet Union, was living an era of cultural homogeneity (and, to some extent, it still is).

"The Elmu association had been founded in 1978 to serve a real need. There simply wasn't any live music in Helsinki."

Lepakko quickly became a stage for diverse music subcultures – punks, rockers, and the decadently avant-garde Bela Lugosi Club – and also for independent publishers, literary circles, movie clubs and artists. It was the place that introduced graffiti and skateboarding to Helsinki. Over its 20 years of existence, Lepakko hosted hundreds and hundreds of underground concerts. Many of the bands would go on to gain cult status or achieve major success. *The Sugarcubes* (Björk), *Sonic Youth* and *Pennywise* are just some of the bands that reached Finland via Lepakko.

Graffiti depicting "pohjanoteeraus" (rock bottom) and "Tapio Rautavaara" (the legendary Finnish singer, actor and athlete) on Lepakko's wall raised concerns among passers-by in 1980. Photo: Anja Salmela. Next page: The "Ballet Pathetique," led by choreographer Jorma Uotinen, rehearsing at Cable Factory in 1989. Photo: Stefan Bremer

Radio Breakthrough

In 1985, Lepakko witnessed the birth of the oldest (still operational) commercial radio station in Finland, *Radio City*. Up until then there had been a radio monopoly in Finland. The Finnish state broadcaster, *Yleisradio*, was broadcasting two alternative channels plus some Swedish programming. Teemu Lehto, Elmu's visionary, came up with the idea of starting a radio station for young people.

Kimmo Helistö was among Radio City's first DJ's. "It's difficult to understand today, but the idea of independent radio was totally revolutionary. There wasn't anything else except for national radio. Before Radio City, hardly any rock music was playing on Finnish radio."

Helistö got caught up in Lepakko activities and even worked as chairman of Elmu from 1989-92 and later as a doorman at *Höyryklubi* (Steam club) – the club that combined saunas and nightclub music, led by *DJ Tixa*.

"It was an astounding achievement that the city allowed Lepakko to continue for 20 years. I'm not sure how it was possible. Of course, it was a constant battle and we were often put under pressure to leave the building. Lepakko was able to stay, partly because of Elmu's smart work. For the first few years Elmu was only paying 100 Marks rent per *year* – but of course renovating the house at its own expense."

"The city's attitude was more permissive than it is today," says Lehto, who himself took part in many other successful squats during the 1980's. "Nowadays the city would order the police to take care of squatters."

In 1999 however, Lepakko was demolished and replaced by a high tech center following the construction of the adjacent *Ruoholahti* residential district. The building may have disappeared but the seeds of new culture and new networks had nevertheless been planted.

> *"The idea of independent radio was totally revolutionary. There wasn't anything else except for national radio."*

Powered by internationalization and more open relations with Western Europe, the streams of marginal cultures that sprung from Lepakko quickly became mainstream. So-called "city culture" started to rampage from the mid-1980's onwards. Accelerated by the booming economy, new independent media outlets, such as Radio City, and the local free newspaper *City*, represented new values of freedom, individuality and modern multiculturalism.

After the political activism of the 1960's and 1970's, the new cultural rebellion was free from politics – it was social rather than societal. The new ethos, as described in the book *City on sinun* (The City is Yours, 2000) was: "Let's find sponsors, organize funding and start a new magazine, radio station, restaurant, or a design shop." [2]

Things were starting to develop from the bottom up, even though Finnish society was traditionally strongly reliant on a conventional political system.

From Cables to Culture

"I was raised into the active community culture of the 1980's and I think it's great the same attitude is making a comeback," rejoices

architect **Pia Ilonen**. She was a leading figure in the cultural take-over of Nokia's old cable factory at the beginning of the 1990's, roughly ten years after Lepakko was founded.

Helsinki's *Kaapelitehdas* (Cable Factory) is one of the biggest cultural factories in Europe, with 55,000 square meters of cultural space. It has been running since 1991 – long enough that locals take its existence for granted.

In 1989, Ilonen had seen a newspaper ad: "Workspaces rented for a year." Nokia was quitting its old factory in Ruoholahti – the company's success in mobile technology was yet to be foreseen.

"We told our friends, who told their friends, and within a month the whole building was occupied by art and culture," Ilonen recalls. "The new tenants got to build their own premises in the large halls. We decided to find out what was going to happen to these unique spaces after our contract ended."

The Cable Factory's courtyard with an old cable drum. Kirsi Monni is pictured dancing on the roof.
Photos: Stefan Bremer, 1989

It turned out that in the new masterplan for Ruoholahti, the factory was planned to be demolished. The tenants quickly founded the *Pro Kaapeli* movement to argument against the plans, with Ilonen at the forefront.

"I started making an alternative proposal for the city. Soon another architect, **Jan Verwijnen**, who had experience from the Netherlands, rang the doorbell and wanted to join. Our main argument was a 'do nothing policy.' Besides the unique factory building, we wanted to protect the community and networks that had already been created. We pointed out flaws in the masterplan and made suggestions for rearranging the functions in order to preserve the cable factory."

After one-and-a-half years of seemingly endless negotiations with the City of Helsinki and a flurry of media coverage, the city was ready to cooperate. Ilonen recalls: "I compared the process with a space ship determined to move towards its doom. I can't describe the feeling when the ship slowly started to turn. Then the press came to support us. And finally, the economic downturn at the beginning of the 1990's made it clear: what we needed was already there – no other investments were necessary."

Cable Factory today is a well functioning machine comprising artists' studios, sports facilities, small-scale manufacturing, small museums and spaces for events, from big concerts and dance performances to design fairs. In the last 20 years the building has been renovated little by little, with a light touch.

"It is actually a miracle that the so-called 'SoHo phenomenon' hasn't taken place here –

where artists have been followed by gallerists and entrepreneurs, with prices getting higher and the artists having to find a new location. Instead Kaapeli has lasted as it is because of foresight and good strategic decision-making," Ilonen concludes.

After Cable Factory, new cultural locations have been founded in Helsinki's old tram halls and power plants. Run by the same organization as Cable Factory, since 2008, the 100-year-old *Suvilahti* power plant has worked as a barren but beautiful urban stage for events, such as the *Flow Festival*.

One of Helsinki's most trailblazing venues unfortunately had the same destiny as Lepakko. Between 1989 and 2006, the old central railway warehouses, known as *Makasiinit*, were a provocative hotspot for urban subculture that even got to function as the official living room for Helsinki's year as European Capital of Culture in 2000. Since 2011, the brand new Helsinki Music Centre has stood in their place. After the demolition verdict in 2006, parts of the Makasiinit were "accidentally" burned down – for as yet unknown reasons.[3]

Towards the "Paradise City"

The battle against apathy is still raging in 2012, although it is being manifested in more celebratory forms. The success of events like Restaurant Day *(see p.140)*, shows that people are motivated by doing concrete things that have an impact – however temporary – on their environment. Soft criticism of the city's bureaucracy is being channeled into urban gardens and street parties. People are learning to use their city in more creative ways. However, those who are willing to pursue new ideas may still have to be prepared for long duels with bureaucracy.

Kimmo Helistö, today a local politician and entrepreneur, points out: "There is so much potential in youth and alternative culture, which is not properly acknowledged. Young people have incredible power – and they can learn a lot from doing things with others. I refer to Lepakko as my university and business school. I learned networking and organization skills, marketing, graphic design – all as a side effect of all that punk rock nonsense."

"We told our friends, who told their friends, and within a month the whole complex was occupied by art and culture."

"Mr. Lepakko," Teemu Lehto, hasn't lost his passion for cities and culture. One of his current plans is to create an urban garden at the top of the 1930's *Lasipalatsi* ("The Glass Palace") at the very heart of Helsinki. He also wants to fill the adjacent square with fruit trees. "There would be apples, pears and cherry trees, which would all blossom at different times," Lehto envisions.

"We should endeavor to make our city a paradise – otherwise it may turn into an 'empire of greed.' It's entirely up to us to decide what kind of city we want to live in." With living experience of the subject, Lehto points out that genuine urban culture is born from the grassroots on a local level. "I want to work on ideas that are positive and have a social dimension – ideas that make people strive towards the 'paradise city' together."

---

1 Lindfors, Jukka; Salo, Markku (1988). *Nupit kaakkoon – Elmu 10 vuotta*. Helsinki: Elävän musiikin yhdistys ry.

Rantanen, Miska (2000). *Lepakkoluola*. Helsinki: Wsoy

2 Isokangas, Antti; Karvala, Kaappo; Von Reiche, Markus (2000). *City on sinun – kuinka uusi kaupunkikulttuuri tuli Helsinkiin*. Helsinki: Tammi.

3 Oksanen, Kimmo (2006). *Makasiinit 1899-2006*. Helsinki: Helsingin Sanomat.

Hello From the Future

The Clues to Open Helsinki project explored a range of possibilities for a more engaged and participatory future. Materialized as a set of postcards from the future sent out to city officials and local leaders in 2010, the project by creative practice OK Do and Sitra proposed concrete steps for carrying out new ideas. Here are a few greetings from a future Helsinki.

TEXT: OK DO AND BRYAN BOYER / SITRA · ILLUSTRATIONS: NENE TSUBOI

Katu Mayors

Katu ("street" in Finnish) Mayors live in their own neighborhood and are elected by their peers. They participate in neighborhood-level planning and ensure that residents and local organizations are heard, breathing diversity into different pockets of the city. These local trustees are supported by grants and are involved in local permitting, which allows them to manage the environment, services and facilities.

Urbane Industry

Few places have a craft legacy as strong as Finland. Today, local talent has been saved from the brink of extinction through programs that encourage and foster small-scale industry in the heart of the city. Multicultural skills merge as designers and manufacturers collaborate closely together.

Winter Holidays

Helsinki's unique seasonal circumstances are newly appreciated, due to part of the long summer holiday period being moved to winter. People cherish the value in cold and short Helsinki days as they discover places that encourage them to stay in the city and meet up in winter, just as they do in summer. Wouldn't a winter garden be a nice place to while away winter days? In addition to holidays, new urban ski tracks are open along pedestrian routes, allowing people to ski from home to work, avoiding the gridlock of icy roads.

Working Together

Helsinki's freelancers are flourishing thanks to a new variety of "third place" venues. These are neither home or traditional office, but offer a more casual environment, which can flow easily from socializing to working. As flexible spaces they are also alive after hours and on weekends. In the summer they spill outside onto terraces and parks and, in the winter, they are places where one can enjoy a hot cup of tea over inspiring conversations.

A City of All Shapes and Sizes

The city is built from the bottom up. There is more variation in the urban pattern: small townhouses, bigger complexes, and new and old buildings sit next to each other. Communal housing is becoming popular and people combine living and working under the same roof. A lotting system has been introduced to distribute urban spaces to different organizations, giving more freedom for individual builders while opening up the city plan to new commercial and social interests.

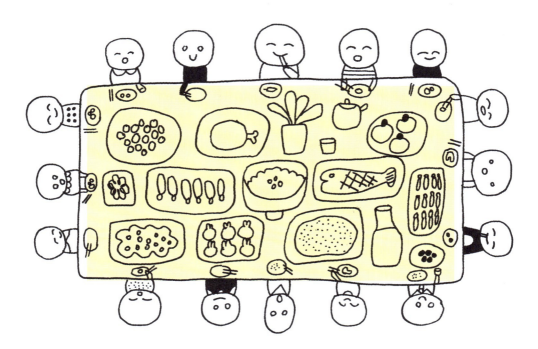

Sharing Cultures by Sharing Meals

Food has become a safe first step towards increasing Helsinki's multiculturalism. Sharing meals with and from other cultures has opened up news doors of understanding. At the moment, a new Sudanese restaurant and Helsinki's first Brazilian coffee shop are competing for the title of the most popular casual restaurant in the city. With the help of good recipes from overseas, the new "Vege Day" at Helsinki schools and kindergartens has become one of the most popular lunch options.

↳ *www.cluestoopenhelsinki.com*

Helsinki Internationals

Finnish art, culture and science have been recognized internationally since the times of Albert Edelfelt, Jean Sibelius and Alvar Aalto. Helsinki wouldn't be the place it is without the new ideas that are born when cultures mix. Yet Finland is known for its reserved attitude towards foreign cultural influences and immigration. We asked six citizens of the world, who call Helsinki their home, to share their views on the city.

TEXT: HELLA HERNBERG · PHOTOS: JOHANNES ROMPPANEN

Less than half the people in Helsinki were born here. Many of us have arrived from other parts of Finland or from around the world. Helsinki was a much smaller town until the mass migration of people in search for work from the countryside started after the World Wars.

On a global scale Helsinki has relatively few inhabitants of foreign origin, representing roughly ten percent of the population. However, 90 percent of the city's current population growth is based on immigrants and their children. The largest foreign language groups in 2008 were Russian, Estonian, Somali, English, Arabic and Chinese.[1]

After being geographically isolated for centuries, Helsinki is now an international air traffic junction, a transit gateway between Asian metropolises and Western cities.

Helsinki's internationalization has been accelerating since 1995 when Finland joined the EU. Before that, the collapse of Soviet Union in the early 1990's brought a big wave of immigrants to Finland. Even at the beginning of the 20th century, the proportion of residents born abroad was as large as it is today. Many traditionally "Finnish" enterprises, such as Stockmann and Fazer, were founded in the 19th century by immigrants or their offspring.[2]

Immigration has recently raised a lot of media attention, which has polarized public opinion. Researcher **Sirkku Varjonen** has studied immigrants' life stories and identities.

"Debate is a good thing, but it is important to really listen to the needs of different parties,

Wisam Elfadl: "Over the 20 years I have lived in Helsinki it has grown more heterogeneous – even in its western areas. Still, I'd hope for a greater cultural mix. I also have a feeling that a stronger sense of locality and a stronger feeling of community are coming."

both local and foreign, and to find where their needs create synergies. There are lots of similarities in people's daily lives, regardless of their nationality or background."

Varjonen suggests that acceptance of differences on a local level usually benefits everyone and leads to a more comfortable and welcoming atmosphere in general. As a good example she mentions the *Refugee Hospitality Club*, an open volunteer network that was started in autumn 2009, when new reception centers for asylum seekers were opened in the *Punavuori* and *Kallio* districts of Helsinki. Their aim is to make these neighborhoods feel more like villages where guests from around the world can feel welcome.

"For those who don't want a regular office job, the potential to create something is great but you have to be exceptionally focused and willing to get to your goal." – GARETH HAYES

But why do people actually want to move to a city on the periphery of Europe – a place where, for much of the year, you have to survive through slush, wind and freezing temperatures?

Varjonen mentions that increasingly, decisions to move here are driven by other factors than necessity: "Many people move to Finland for love. Work, curiosity, studies, and creative independence have also brought immigrants to Helsinki, in the same way that they have inspired others, including intrepid Finns, to explore different parts of the world."

We talked with six interesting personalities from various backgrounds, for whom Helsinki has become home. Many of them appreciate the close presence of nature, Helsinki's small scale and the well-functioning society – things that native Finns can easily take for granted. For visual artist **Sasha Huber**, long winters allow concentration on work and detail. Parents of small children, such as Huber or **Tatiana Pertseva**, praise Helsinki as a family friendly and safe city. **Ian Bourgeot** and **Gareth Hayes** have added to Helsinki's cultural offerings by running their own businesses. And as designer and passionate cyclist **Jeremiah Tesolin** says: "The scale of Helsinki is such that you can get many things done in one day without taking so much time on transportation. I find it a luxury, both for work and private life."

Even today's cosmopolites live their lives locally. Cities and neighborhoods should be places where diverse cultures can live side by side. Our interviewees all shared the concern that Helsinki should become more multicultural and welcoming.

As **Wisam Elfadl** puts it: "I hope that in the future, the cultural mix adds more audacity to Finnish traits, so you can no longer tell who is 'native' Finnish."

---

1 *Immigration and Immigrants in Helsinki – Statistics, City of Helsinki.* City of Helsinki Urban Facts 2/2010

2 Leitzinger, Antero (2008). *Ulkomaalaiset Suomessa 1812-1972.* Helsinki: East-West Books

Re-Imagining Helsinki 49

Clockwise from top left: Bookseller **Ian Bourgeot** is glad that at the Arkadia International Bookshop people have found rare books they have been looking for for a long time. Visual artist **Sasha Huber** enjoys the natural patches of greenery in the city center, like this spot by Töölö bay. Designer **Jeremiah Tesolin** used to race at a high level and is still a passionate cyclist. He appreciates the small scale of Helsinki, which makes it easy and efficient to move around. For art project coordinator **Tatiana Pertseva** the Linnanmäki amusement park is a place of rest where people become more open and friendly. (See the interviews, pp.52-53)

Wisam Elfadl
STUDENT OF CULTURAL PRODUCTION

"We came to Helsinki from Sudan when I was five for my father's university studies. I live in Kallio with my Finnish husband.

We visit Sudan once or twice a year and, while I'm away, I miss Finnish public transport and privacy. Back here I long for Sudanese arrogance and spontaneity. People there are more laid-back. Despite poverty people don't worry too much about how much money they have in their pockets.

The Sudanese concept of home is much wider than in Finland – it extends to the garden and the street. Even in Helsinki my territory changes like a Barbapapa and it includes the market square, the small shops, the shoemaker's and the African hairdressers.

There is a big African-Finnish community living in Helsinki. Although "African" is a very wide concept, it's really what unites us living here. People keep an eye on each other and organize big parties. Still, it's a pity that the native and African cultural groups don't really mix. The media also leave our culture rather in secret – except for the negative news about crime, rapes and so on.

"The native and African culture groups don't really mix. The media also leave our culture rather in secret – except for all the negative news."

Of course, stereotypes exist both ways. I was prejudiced about Finnish men who, in my opinion, behave like boys until 35. And yet, here I am, married to one! On the other hand, for Africans it's important to be social. For the men hanging around the railway station it can be an important social activity, though it may seem dubious to others."

Gareth Hayes
INDEPENDENT PRODUCER

"I was born in North London but my family roots go further to Wales, Mauritius and Ireland. I studied in Britain and in Lapland, and lived for a while in Berlin before moving to Helsinki in 2002.

With friends we started a small independent gallery and shop project called Myymälä2. The idea was to provide an alternative for less established artists and craftsmen to launch their careers. Being at the gallery rapidly introduced me to a lot of people and I settled in.

The gallery developed very quickly from a side-project to our main focus, and in large part that's due to all the people who came to us either to help out or to create exhibitions and projects. I gained a lot of valuable experience, although as an informal organization we had our challenges too, mostly from the business side.

When we first started Myymälä2 we were considering the Kallio district, but thought it would have been too out of the way. In the last two to three years, there have been great spaces attracting audiences further out. The Ptarmigan gallery space near the old rail yards in Vallila is a good example.

One of the things I value most in Finland is the support for culture. I guess part of that is because of the size of the population, but it feels much more accessible here.

When it comes to work, I've found the atmosphere in Helsinki to be twofold. For those who don't want a regular office job, the potential to create something is great, but you have to be exceptionally focused and willing to develop the infrastructure to get to your goal. Ultimately that's not a terrible thing, but slightly better support and more nurturing would turn what is good into something exceptional."

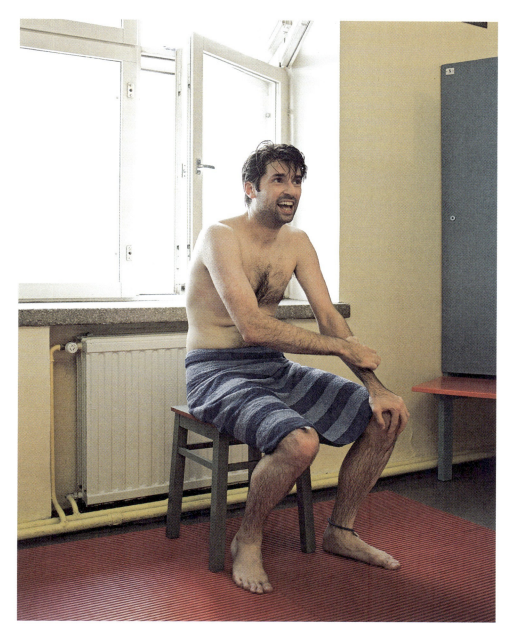

Gareth Hayes: "I've been a fan of *sauna* for a long time now, particularly the social aspect. Public saunas here provide neutral territory for a broad range of people and it's a place where Finnish men feel like they can talk freely. I've lived close to the *Arla Sauna* for over seven years and the mix of people that run the place, the location, and of course, the quality of the löyly, make it quite unique."

Ian Bourgeot
BOOKSELLER AND TEACHER

"I was born in London in 1962. My mother was from Guatemala City and my father was Parisian. I lived on all five continents before moving to Finland in 1993.

I'm married with three children and came to Finland with my first wife, a Finn. The atmosphere was more relaxed than other places I knew – with a high degree of tolerance and liberty for personal expression. As a language teacher I utterly failed to learn Finnish or Swedish, but that hasn't prevented me from living a good life here and running two enterprises.

In 2008, I founded the *Arkadia International Bookshop* in *Töölö*. I had never imagined opening a bookshop. I simply had a large collection of books, which I thought I could live without. It was an unwise idea in so many ways – in the midst of the Internet revolution. Even so, it was one of the very best decisions I ever made. I would never have met my new wife otherwise.

"I value Finnish humour, gentleness, curiosity, intelligence and the voluntaristic approach to life, balanced with much common sense."

In the bookshop I have met extraordinary minds and passionate people of all ages, sexes and opinions. We've also hosted a large range of cultural events from poetry and music to monologues and magic.

I only miss things that are quite impossible to recover: Mexican ice-creams at Plaza del Sol in Guadalajara, playing as a child in Kensington Gardens, the forgotten cinemas of Paris, walks in rubber plantations in Malaysia...

Honestly, I'm quite content living in Finland. I value Finnish humor, gentleness, curiosity, intelligence and the voluntaristic approach to life, balanced with much common sense. Life is challenging as a whole, and Finland has been rather considerate and helpful to me."

Sasha Huber
VISUAL ARTIST

"I've always been fascinated by history and my roots, which are mainly based in Switzerland and Haiti.

My husband, who's from Helsinki, introduced me to Finland. We met in 2000 in Italy at Benetton's creative lab, Fabrica, and decided to move to Helsinki. I was open to moving to a new city without knowing much about it.

"Finnish traditions and practices relating to nature, design and technology are inspirational – almost magical."

Together with **Petri**, we have our own studio and work in visual art and design. We also have a small son, **Basil**. Young families like ours try to hang on in the city rather than move out into the periphery even though rents are very expensive.

Petri discovered a good exhibition space in our house in 2007 when we moved back to Kallio. It took four years for *Kallio Kunsthalle* (KaKu) to be realized. KaKu is a pocket of art in the heart of Kallio – a product of artists, scholars and local associations. Petri directs the artistic social work and I run daily tasks and help out.

As Helsinki has become my second home I've become influenced by its history. For example, my interest in the Finnish artist **Akseli Gallen-Kallela** relates to his African safari and the hunting of animals that was common in the 1900's. He left his home country to experience the world and brought back memories that challenged local perspectives.

Helsinki has been an ideal place for me to develop and invest my life in. I think Finnish traditions and practices relating to nature, design and technology are inspirational – almost magical. The long winters feel similar to Switzerland. Being surrounded by the cold, snow and mountains, one can concentrate on work and details."

Tatiana Pertseva
ART PROJECT COORDINATOR

"I was born in Petrozavodsk, the capital of the Karelian republic, and studied there in the Russian Academy of Science. In 1998, we moved with my husband to Joensuu in Eastern Finland. We studied the Finnish language together and I gave birth to my second child in 1999. My first baby had died in Russia at the age of three weeks.

We moved to Helsinki in 2002 and I started to study IT and then Russian literature. Between my studies I worked as a bartender and art-project coordinator.

In Helsinki I have met with creative and cheerful people, with whom we started to gather together to share interesting news, and to read and write poetry and short stories in Russian. With our association, Studia Litera, we've also organized music events and festivals – one of them was a concert by the famous Moscow dark-folk band Rada i Ternovik in 2006.

Ecological thinking is important to me. In Helsinki and Finland, I especially value clean air and water and how the social system works. I also really enjoy the fact that many Finns are fond of sports. Then again, people's reticence and psychological distance are what I don't really like.

"In general I don't think communities or circles can be based only on nationality. An educated person who wants to learn more about the world should always find a common language with other people."

In general I don't think communities or circles can be based only on nationality. An educated person who wants to learn more about the world should always find a common language with other people."

Jeremiah Tesolin
DESIGNER

"Some say 70% of immigrants move to Finland for love and I'm one of those. When I moved here in 2000, Helsinki was a curious place that was getting a lot of attention with the rise of Nokia, the new media scene, Bombfunk MC's, and design.

I honestly thought I would be here for a couple of years but one thing led to another. After freelance work, a bankrupt IT startup, work at Nokia, and an MA, I also met my wonderful wife, made two boys, and now work at Marimekko. That's 12 years and counting.

"Still in Helsinki city, yet with a forest in front of our house where we can ski, run, bike, and pick blueberries in the summer."

I'm originally from St. Catharines in Ontario, Canada, a small city labeled as the 'doughnut capital of the world.' We just moved to Paloheinä in northern Helsinki – an amazing place – still in Helsinki city, yet with a forest in front of our house where we can ski, run, bike, and pick blueberries in the summer.

Helsinki's small scale, the proximity to nature, and the variety of indoor and outdoor activities, are all important to me. There's a good balance here between work and private life and I consider living in Helsinki to be extremely efficient.

I used to race at a high level in Canada and I still ride competitively. There are a lot of diverse routes in Helsinki. Within 20 minutes you're in the countryside with bicycle paths along all the busy roads.

Still, I'd hope that Finland and Helsinki would be able to take advantage of the influx of immigrants. Foreign influences should help evolve the Finnish identity rather than taking anything away from it. I've lived 12 years in Finland, have a family of four 'Tesolins' and I am still considered a foreigner. I call myself a 'non-native' Finn."

2. Everyman's Urbanism

In the forests of Finland people enjoy "everyman's rights." Helsinki citizens have translated this tradition into a new urban attitude. People and communities are engaging in developing the city's corners into better places and Helsinki is becoming a more enjoyable and inspiring hometown.

Home Street Home

An artist wanted to do something to make Helsinki a nicer place. She started with her home street. And Punajuuri Block Party was born.

TEXT: HETA KUCHKA · PHOTOS: TANI SIMBERG

The text on my phone's screen says: "Delivered to **Jimi Tenor**." Now I'm really nervous. What's he going to say? I'm sitting on a blanket in my garden, fingers crossed. My cat, **Babar**, circles around me, making pitstops in my lap every once in a while before retreating back to his little jungle behind our yard. Babar is on summer vacation. I'm not as lucky. Ok, now I have to call all the other musicians on my list. And I really have to talk to **Reijo** the policeman.

Over the past couple of years my art has dealt with how we live and die here in Helsinki. There's more and more loneliness in the city. And we also treat each other worse. The "I don't need anyone" mentality has become the norm.

I started hanging out at morgues, and going to the funerals of lonely people with no friends or family, to learn about life. I decided I wanted to do something to make this city a nicer place to live. I started with my street, *Pursimiehenkatu*.

Saturday, 3 September 2011. Punajuuri Block Party. I make my way to the front row and plant myself at the end of a line of little girls sitting on the trolley tracks. I slowly scan the crowd of over two thousand people. Men and women of all ages are visibly moved as they watch the dramatic performance by the world's most street credible dance troupe, the *Wannabe Ballerinas*.

Less than five minutes ago I was still talking my way out of what could have been a sticky situation with the three police cars that pulled up right before the show was supposed to start. Now the air hangs heavy with anticipation and pure joy. For the first time ever, Helsinki's *Viiskulma* intersection has been completely taken over by pedestrians, and it's all ours for the next two hours. I've been waiting for this moment for so long. Six months of grueling, non-stop volunteer work has totally paid off. And now my old friends, thousands of new ones and I, get to share the *Bad Ass Brass Band* and Jimi Tenor gigs together.

"For the first time ever, Helsinki's Viiskulma intersection has been completely taken over by pedestrians, and it's all ours for the next two hours."

K-X-P (middle, left), Diop Momar from the band Mama Africa (bottom, left) and the Bad Ass Brass Band (bottom, right) entertaining the crowds at the Punajuuri Block Parties of 2010 and 2011.

Punajuuri's creators, Flavor Flav (left, middle) and Chuck D (left, below), partying to the Wannabe Ballerinas (right, middle) amongst others.

I'd been thinking about organizing a block party for a while. *Punavuori* literally translates into "Red Hill," so when my old elementary school friend, **Jon**, came up with the name *Punajuuri* (Beetroot), we knew it was the perfect name for a party that was also a celebration of our own roots.

We threw the first "house party" in fall 2010, and the reception we got was amazing. Our aliases, *Chuck D* and *Flavor Flav*, still argue with each other like they have since first grade, but it's just as much fun as it used to be.

"Six months of grueling, non-stop volunteer work has totally paid off."

Arif and **Nicke** got busy (as hell), and they did a great job dealing with all our craziness. The "dog park gang" were put on balloon duty under **Siru**'s steady leadership. The string of bright, beautiful balloons was draped from the Schnauzer's window to the Labrador's window and ended at the Dachshund's place.

I met lots of new people just by standing around my corner, the place to be, with **Keitsi** the ex-firefighter. Some of our neighbors decided to sponsor us by donating the proceeds of a backyard flea market and pop-up hand-rolled sushi shop. **Tani** and **Meri** came into my life with their cameras and a picnic basket, right as we were about to start our Punajuuri t-shirt fashion shoot with **Ritva**, the French Bulldog puppy.

And Pastor **Teemu** came to the rescue when we were in desperate need of a sound system for our stage. "Jesus has your back," he said. And with that he invited us to open a pop-up restaurant that we ran out of the church's windows.

Severi had just moved back to the old neighborhood, and he and his wife **Tea** were sitting at an outdoor table at the *Ankkuri* bar making plans for their anniversary. It only took about 10 minutes for them to get bitten by the Punajuuri bug. "I mean, we can go out to a romantic dinner some other night. So would 20 LED lights be enough?" Thanks to these light designer lovebirds, a dark and dreary fall night turned into a brilliant light show, disco balls and all. They celebrated their anniversary with about 8,000 other people to the rhythm of *Gracias* and *Accu*.

I've lived in Punavuori all my life. As a child old men used to tell me wild stories about the old days when they made their dates walk home alone from Viiskulma because of the neighborhood's bad reputation.

When I had tantrums as a kid, I'd escape to the little grocery store on *Albertinkatu*. I loved the grocer. He gave me free candy because my mom had forced me to go in and apologize for stealing candy. My friends and I played in the local parks we nicknamed *Koffari* and *Seppäri*. As teenagers we got drunk at the little kiosk in *Eira*. Nowadays our local coffee place, *Kaffecentralen*, is the neighborhood "adult daycare center."

One of the brightest parts of everyday life in Punavuori is **Eeva Kanerva**'s used bookstore, where one of my cats works. He socializes with the customers and cheers people up as they pass by the shop window and see him perched on his pile of books. It's a great place to go when you want to escape the fall darkness. I popped in last week and Eeva handed me a copy of the *Hufvudstadsbladet* newspaper. It said: "Pursimiehenkatu – The hippest street in town."

Let The Beet Go On… YEAH BOYYYYY!

↳ *www.punajuuri.org*

The City as I Want to See It

An art student challenges conventional notions about media messages in public urban space with three remarkable and touching creations.

TEXT: ELISSA ERIKSSON

The October afternoon sun is shining across the railway yard. I'm eyeing the mesh fence that separates *Kaisaniemi Park* from the multitude of tracks that lead to Helsinki's Central Railway Station. I'm going to use the fence as my canvas and I'm considering what font size to use.

The idea of leaving messages in urban public space formed gradually in my mind. The initial spark came at the beginning of my art education studies. During a media pedagogy course I realized that verbal and visual messages flood the city.

This observation led me to regard the urban space as one medium alongside all the others, though different in a certain aspect. I receive messages in the urban space without having any choice in whether I wish to receive them or not.

When I started my studies at the beginning of the 2000's, Helsinki was in the middle of a debate about graffiti, street art and the *Stop Töhryille* anti-graffiti campaign. I reflected on the matter from the media perspective. If urban space were a medium that every urban *flâneur* is inevitably subjected to, wouldn't it be important for it to contain as diverse a range of messages as possible – and perhaps even opportunities to interact?

Unfortunately, the public discussion about street art seemed to be limited to questions of legality/illegality. Annoyed, I started developing

Photo: Sebastian Greger

Work in progress with autumn leaves in Ruskeasuo, Helsinki. Photo: Elissa Eriksson.
Next page: The text "After all, this is my city" standing on a fence in Kaisaniemi park. Photo: Sebastian Greger

tools and ideas for anyone willing to legally make their message visible in the urban space. This toying with ideas finally resulted in the subject of my artistic thesis: finding and testing ways to leave messages in the city.

Standing by the fence next to the rail tracks, I was about to embark on my first experiment.

After All, This Is My City

"What does it say?" "It's definitely not vandalism!" "At least the city won't have to spend money cleaning that up."

Passers-by comment on my work, and many people smile and give me "the thumbs up" as I place leaves into the holes in the mesh fence. After two afternoons, colorful fall leaves form a sentence that can be seen by train passengers, as well as by people who walk through the park.

"Tämä on kuitenkin minun kaupunkini" (After all, this is my city) is a quote from the Zen Café song, Minun kaupunkini (My city). For me, the statement crystallizes something essential about my affection for my current hometown.

> "The public discussion about street art seemed to be limited to questions of legality/illegality. Annoyed, I started developing tools and ideas for anyone willing to legally make their message visible in the urban space."

With the help of the song, I wanted to post my "Like" message visibly in our city, in such a way that no one could accuse me of littering or damaging someone else's property. The fall leaves proved to be fine writing material. Packed into big enough bunches and squeezed into the fence holes, the leaves stayed in place without any other adhesive materials.

The reactions of passers-by in Kaisaniemi Park were so encouraging that I decided to continue writing the message in two other places. The fence next to *Kalasatama* metro station was quite different to the one in the park. No one interrupted my work with questions or comments. Afterwards I found a photo online with the comment: "After all, this is my city – that's what it says but it was hard to get a shot of. And I was rushing for the metro. Nice gesture from those who did this. Thank you!"

In *Ruskeasuo*, opposite the *Tilkka* hospital, I wrote the message on a fence that marks the boundary of a residential building's yard along the *Mannerheimintie* main road. Some of the building's residents stopped for a chat. One of them said that the message was a welcome alternative to the advertising boards that often cover the wall of the hospital across the road.

I Want to See Something Else

I'm standing at a tram stop staring at a poster advertisement while November snowflakes float down from the sky. Suddenly a question pops into my head: what if I wanted to post my message here? Could I, just like any company representative, march into the outdoor advertising company's office and announce that I want my message posted in the urban space? The price would certainly be too high for one person, but what if the space was rented as a team effort? Perhaps it would be possible to make it clear that we want to see something else, not just ads, in our city streets.

"I want to see humanity and authenticity." "I want to see new Finnish comic art." "I want to see drawings by children." "I want to see more nature!" "I want to see things without a price tag." "I want to see these words: 'You are good just as you are.'"

Only two months have passed since I started developing the thought of jointly renting advertising space at tram and bus stops – an idea that seemed crazy at the time. Now I'm standing again at a tram stop looking at the poster. It is covered in over 1,300 small messages where as many people are saying what they would like to see in their urban space.

> *"I'm standing at a tram stop staring at a poster advertisement while November snowflakes float down from the sky. Suddenly a question pops into my head: what if I wanted to post my message here?"*

The pattern made up of the tiny messages forms a background for the project's title, *Haluan nähdä muutakin* (I Want to See Something Else). The writing at the bottom of the poster explains: "1,458 people wanted to liberate this space from commercial messages for one week."

Above: The "I Want to See Something Else" poster on a tram stop in front of the railway station. Photo: Elissa Eriksson
Below: Guests reading the messages on the poster at the opening party. Photo: Juha Snellman

One of the "Home Lights" ice lanterns on the Senate square. Photo: Elissa Eriksson

A Small Idea and a Big Effort

My idea had quickly become reality. Initially I had found out that the minimum number of poster sites we'd have to rent was 21. The cost of this package – almost 6,000 Euros – sounded unrealistically high but I decided to try and make it happen with the help of Facebook. I calculated that 1,000 participants would be enough – if they each invested roughly the cost of a pizza.

Word about the "I want to see something else" effort spread fast and, within a few weeks, the Facebook page had several thousand "Likes." The required sum was collected in a matter of weeks and there would have been many more willing participants. The media also covered the project. A journalist first contacted me three days after the Facebook page was published and, over the next two months, I made about a dozen magazine, radio and TV interviews.

The success of the project was overwhelming. Why did the idea of renting advertising space at twenty tram and bus stops excite thousands of people and make news headlines in leading national TV channels and newspapers?

One participant posted this comment on the Facebook page: "Oh yes! I've dreamt of something like this for a long time!" Maybe the project revealed that many people are genuinely interested in interacting and influencing urban spaces but most feel they lack the tools to do it.

Home Lights

I am walking along the Hakaniemi Bridge on a freezing February day with ice lanterns in both hands. A woman passing by notices me and says: "These are lovely. I was wondering who would welcome us like this?" That week had seen several freezing days and most of the ice lanterns I had taken to different parts of the city had stayed in good condition. I'd just gone to light new candles every day. As I place new lanterns on the side of the bridge, a middle-aged couple walks by. When they reach me, the man says three words without breaking his stride: "Thanks for these."

My earlier urban experiments had focused on written messages but I had become interested in the meaning created by acts and objects. Ice and candles were as harmless as materials as fall leaves. In my childhood, ice lanterns dotted the yards in our neighborhood, signaling that people were home and welcoming guests. What would ice lanterns communicate in the middle of the city?

"I was surprised by the strong emotions that stirred in me. The gesture seemed to offer a strong expression of affection and care."

I placed lanterns outside the Central Railway Station and, when one broke when it fell out of my sled, I put it back together and placed it in the Senate Square. When I lit the candle of the first ice lantern in the midst of the rush at the railway station, I was surprised by the strong emotions that stirred in me. The gesture seemed to offer a strong expression of affection and care. Perhaps the message of caring can be read in the lanterns that are left twinkling in the streets on their own.

We Are The City

What did these three urban experiments teach me? Most of all I cherish the supportive and enthusiastic comments from passers-by and participants. It is as if I had fulfilled some collective wish by placing ordinary residents' messages in the urban space. Perhaps people's creativity could be more meaningfully expressed in the streets if they were just given the opportunity.

Then again, I learned to understand that perhaps the biggest obstacle to interacting with the urban environment was not the lack of legal tools. It was rather an illusion, rooted in my mind, that urban space is like a stage set, always defined by someone else, where I am just a passer-by. The key to enabling active participation lies in redefining the role of the urbanite and challenging our own perceptions of what we can achieve. We are the city.

Selected sources and influences:

Klein, Naomi (2001). *No Logo: No Space, No Choice, No Jobs.* London: Flamingo

Rajanti, Taina: *"Onko kaupungissa tilaa?"* Speech at Kiasma Museum of Modern Art, 12/1/2011

http://improveverywhere.com/

http://theyesmen.org/

http://cargocollective.com/urbanblooz

http://www.streetartutopia.com/

Tango Around Town

Vallilan Tango takes traditional Finnish dances to the strangest places: a neglected park, a tram, a night café and a forest pavilion. Old hits are now moving new generations to rediscover Finnish dance culture.

TEXT: ILPO KIISKINEN, ANTTI ALAVUOTUNKI
PHOTOS: HANNA KOIKKALAINEN, HELI SORJONEN

In the early spring of 2005 in Helsinki's Vallila district, a group of friends were inspired to perform old Finnish tango hits. They soon organized themselves into a band that featured all the important dance orchestra instruments of the 1940s: violin, clarinet, trumpet, accordion, guitar, double bass and drums. They practiced in the basement of one of the quaint wooden houses typical of Vallila.

When a seven-song set was ready the band started itching for a gig.

As *Vappu* (the traditional Finnish May Day celebration) approached, **Antti Alavuotunki**, the founder of the band, and **Heli Sorjonen**, who happened to be new neighbors, decided to invite their friends for a garden party.

A sail from a wooden boat was set up as a canopy and under it the *Vallilan Tango* band played their first gig. The Dutch singer, **Hans Wessels**, interpreted the songs charmingly, although he didn't understand a word of what he sang. When all seven songs had been performed, a harmonium was carried out into the yard and the singing continued until dawn.

> *"When all seven songs had been performed, a harmonium was carried out into the yard and the singing continued until dawn."*

Encouraged by the event's huge success, the band started planning another party. Eager new organizers were found from the ranks of the enthusiastically voiced Vappu revelers. Someone had heard that the *Koitto* Temperance Association had a 100-year-old dance pavillion lying unused on nearby *Lammassaari* (Sheep Island). And thus the end-of-summer party, the *Isle of Sheep* festival, was born. It has since turned into an annual event.

To reach Lammassaari, guests have to walk for 15 minutes along a boardwalk through reeds. In the dark evenings of late summer,

Above: Couples dance at the Vallila Vappu dance in 2008.
Below: The May Day eve event, first started as a small garden party, attracts larger crowds every year.

time-honored dance traditions are followed as closely as possible.

The Isle of Sheep program includes poetry readings, art performances and avant-garde shockers. As the dancing lessons begin, people fill the dance floor. The highlight of the evening is a three-hour dance concert that causes floorboards to groan and the windows to rattle.

> *"The sound system was borrowed from a friend's school and the performers' stage came from a concert hall where an acquaintance worked. Electricity was drawn from the band's basement, where there was also a restroom for the public."*

The year after the initial garden party, the organizers decided to hold the Vappu dance in a small park in Vallila. They formed a cultural association and volunteers were recruited to help organize the party.

The sound system was borrowed from a friend's school and the performers' stage came from a concert hall where an acquaintance worked. Electricity was drawn from the band's basement rehearsal room, where there was also a restroom for the public. A canopy was put together from pipes obtained from a construction equipment rental company. The band's repertoire had expanded — they now played for three hours.

News of the event spread by word of mouth. After a few years, the park got too small and the dance was moved to a bigger park a block away.

In 2011, up to 3,000 urbanites of all ages took part in the sixth Vallila Vappu dance. Lined

Previous page: Volunteer Niina Mäkeläinen sets up a buffet stand for the Vappu park dance 2011. Above: A line of traditional "jenkka" dancing shoots out of the forest pavilion at the Midnight Sun Film Festival in Sodankylä, 2008. Below: The Vallilan Tango orchestra under Lapland's magical midnight sun.

From top left: Vallila inhabitants enjoy the Vappu atmosphere. Volunteers on a break for lunch. An improvised refrigerator is one of the lo-fi innovations typical of the Isle of Sheep festival. Lammassaari's old dance pavilion is the perfect setting for traditional tangos and foxtrots.

The Vallila Vappu dance in 2011. Every year on May Day eve, the unnoticed park wakes up for 5 busy hours, soon going back to sleep for the rest of the year.

by wooden houses, the new park location is only a few hundred meters from the garden where the band played its first gig.

The crowd at the free Vappu dance clean up after themselves. After the band has finished its encore, the guests are handed rakes, garbage bags and shovels. The next day the park is at its best – for the rest of the year it fills up with dog poo, rubbish and weeds.

> "After the band has finished playing its encore, the guests are handed rakes, garbage bags and shovels."

The Isle of Sheep festival almost failed to take place in 2011, as there were not enough volunteers. The organizers shared their concern on Facebook and, within three days, almost 50 people signed up and promised to carry, clean, cook and sell, so that the event could go on.

Vallilan Tango also has a life outside Vappu dances and the Isle of Sheep festival. The band likes to play in the oddest locations. Over the years it has performed in a tram, at the railway station, in sleet at the *Night of the Homeless* event, in a night café for alcoholics, on a river jetty, and in a greenhouse, as well as on a dance platform in the middle of the Lapland forest as part of the *Midnight Sun Film Festival* in *Sodankylä*.

The band's music and the association's events are winning back something that should never have been lost. Why is a charming park empty for most of the year? Why is there not live music on trams every day? ■

Tuomas Is (Still) Here

A grown-up architect contemplates the legitimacy of graffiti yet cannot turn his back on a much-loved hobby.

TEXT: TUOMAS SIITONEN

In the spring of 1987 I begged my parents to let me go to the school disco. When I finally got permission and the night of the event was upon me, I put a plan into action that I'd been working on for a long time. I folded a meticulously drawn sketch into the pocket of my denim jacket and went to get the spray paint cans I'd collected for weeks in my building's garbage room. In the rainy night, me and my friend Onni headed to the *Lauttasaarentie* underpass to paint graffiti for the first time. It was the start of my graffiti hobby, which I've kept up for 25 years, and which has strongly influenced my relationship with the urban space.

My interest had already been sparked the previous summer, when exciting and colorful wall paintings had started appearing around the *Lepakko* underground club on *Porkkalankatu* (see p.36). I used to pass Lepakko on the 65A bus almost every day, and I had gone there a few times just to look at the paintings.

I got off the bus and walked along the old fence, following the tram tracks under the bridge. I was amazed at the paintings, which seemed unbelievably skillful. It was titillating to think that someone had managed to paint that picture overnight and now here I was, looking at it in daylight. Not to mention the excitement brought on by the feeling of being in a wasteland – a place where I was not probably allowed. Gravel grated under my feet, strange wood and creosote smells wafted from old workshops.

I was 12 years old. Now, at the age of 36, those same elements still get me tingling with excitement. I've explored wastelands, railways and backyards around the world hunting for graffiti, photographing and painting. I recently happened to see a documentary, made in 1993, in which I declare I'll paint graffiti art for another two to three years – at most ten. "I doubt I'll be still painting in my 30's." What happened?

Time after time I've become fed up with graffiti culture. I've felt like graffiti hasn't developed stylistically in any direction and that

FTC Lifestyle, 1997. Photo: Fuck The Cops

pointless rules have limited the entire form of expression. Then I've found something new and got excited all over again.

"I was 12 years old. Now, at the age of 36, those aforementioned elements still get me tingling with excitement."

Still, I never got sick of the community aspects of graffiti culture. Back in the day, it was great to be able to call a friend's friend, whose number I'd scrawled on a crumpled piece of paper, from a payphone in the *Gare du Nord* in Paris. These days messages are sent to cryptic Gmail addresses to secure a bed and painting company in Bucharest. Over the years graffiti has developed from a youth subculture in New York to a fashion-phenomenon, a global paint and accessories business, and a subject matter for retrospective art shows.

In Helsinki, graffiti culture, as well as the media and official response to it, have followed developments in the rest of the world. In 1986, pictures and ads in magazines were filled with energetic, colorful teenagers that were beautifying the dreary cityscape. The city of Helsinki seemed to commission graffiti for every youth space and event.

When the "tagging" phenomenon exploded at the end of the 80's and early 90's, the media turned painters into dark, hooded characters that symbolized everything that was wrong with cities. Graffiti culture became a symbol for *malaise* and a gateway to criminality and drugs.

In the new millennium graffiti expression became more diverse and the media's interest was revived. Street art communicated to a broader audience and brought forth a new

Above: The Diamonds Crew poses in the Pasila gallery, 1987.
Below: Poe paints in Kalasatama, 2011. Photos: Tuomas Jääskeläinen

character – an artistically ambitious "Robin Hood type" that painted the city on their own terms, beyond the influence of official institutions.

Currently Helsinki city leaders see certain types of graffiti as a sign of a lively urban subculture that can be highlighted in the city's branding. This is, of course, generalizing to a certain degree – but for someone who has been on the fringes of the phenomenon this whole time, it's been interesting to follow how the situation has evolved.

> *"Street art communicated to a broader audience and brought forth a new character – an artistically ambitious "Robin Hood type" that painted the city on their own terms, beyond the influence of official institutions."*

At the end of the 80's, I was part of Helsinki's second generation of graffiti artists – that were still media darlings. But it was also our generation that became the main culprit of the "graffiti problem" in the 1990's, and suffered the harshest sentences and biggest compensation demands. Coming to the 2010's, the media started to pay attention to the sentences and to the costs of official anti-graffiti campaigns. This led to a more tolerant attitude and to the establishment of several areas dedicated to graffiti art in Helsinki.

Nowadays, the graffiti walls in *Suvilahti* and *Kalasatama* attract tens of painters every day and street art seems to be going through a new revival – at least judging by the reactions of the media and the general public. Painted walls symbolize a lively urban culture and self-motivated action. Painters are allowed to develop their expression in the broad light of day and the public can enjoy the end result.

So, is my dream coming true? Do I want a city in which every wall is colorful and painting is allowed everywhere?

At times I've thought of a graffiti neighborhood where the ground floor of every building is a platform for all types of expression. But despite this, I have to confess that I'm not demanding a city like that and I wouldn't even want it.

When I started painting graffiti the entire city suddenly seemed like an empty canvas and the eye started seeking out good places to paint. There were rooftops, fences and various nooks – places that were visible to many by day but that were easy to paint, in secret, at night. Later I started to see buildings as entities and I realized graffiti didn't always suit them.

There have been many times when I've had a moral crisis and questioned the legitimacy of the entire endeavor. Then I've found myself in an abandoned factory on the outskirts of the city, in some ruined building that embodied decades of political and financial dreams, filled with visual symbols. And to these I can add my own message. The feeling is indescribably empowering.

In this respect, walls raised specifically for painting are literally "thin." Graffiti pieces all in a row lack some of the power that is born from the contrast with the "canvas of context" – of architecture, building materials and history. For me graffiti is not a picture detached from the environment. At its best it is the perfect fracture in its context – an act that transforms a space and challenges people to see things differently. ■

Helsinki Through a Skateboarder's Eye

Shopping for concrete waves in the malls, flea markets and factory shops of an innocent city.

TEXT: VALTTERI VÄKEVÄ · PHOTOS: TUUKKA KAILA

There it is. A small concrete ditch that leads to a garage. It's located right next to *Kasarmikatu*, a street in downtown Helsinki. Most people walk past it without paying any attention to the structure.

If they took a closer look, they might notice that the wall next to it is filled with hundreds of marks left by skateboard wheels.

Whoever first realized that you could use the ditch to ride on the wall had a great skateboarder's eye; the remarkable ability to find unlikely places that can be used for skateboarding.

One could compare this ability to spotting rare design lamps at the flea market. You have to be a true design geek to know their value. You have to look for certain details. And only a small number of people know what those details are.

In the same way that ordinary people don't understand the value of those lamps, non-skateboarders can't imagine the opportunities that the ditch on Kasarmikatu has to offer.

You can't really blame them. Skateboarding was founded on the idea of surfing on dry land, and that ditch certainly doesn't look like a concrete wave. It's more like a splash of cement.

"Then one day you find it; your own un-skated splash of cement. Unfortunately you can't drag it home like a lamp."

The architecture in Helsinki is a weird mixture of concrete brutalism and art nouveau buildings standing shoulder-to-shoulder. It takes a good skateboarder's eye to find new spots in such surroundings.

The functionalist look of this Kasarmikatu skate spot resembles some rare Alvar Aalto stuff you find at flea markets – if you're lucky. And if you're really lucky, you don't break your ankle trying a kickflip wallride on that wall.

Above: The concrete tree pots at Itäkeskus are to skateboarding what the Scaragoo lamp by Stefan Lindfors is to lamp design; a classic with a 1980's / early 1990's vibe.

Right: This skate spot near the Kamppi shopping mall is similar to the Globlow lamps by Valvomo. It looks crazy and is attractive at first glance, but the usability is a bit so-so.

Just like the Italian Barometro lamps, that underpass in Pasila is rough, gloomy and unfinished. You have to be really deep in the game to appreciate such qualities.

One could compare Helsinki Music Centre's yard to Harri Koskinen's Block lamp. It is modern, stylish and clean – but also a bit too popular.

Opposite: This granite block in front of Pasila library is like an office fluorescent light – looks dull but does its job.

Sometimes it's easier, like when a new office building or shopping mall is completed. Finding spots there is like searching for design lamps on eBay. You can at least expect to find something, but the joy of discovery is not that great. And you know that hundreds of others are fishing in the same waters.

Then there are the back alleys and abandoned industrial areas; the flea markets of skateboarding. They are challenging and many times you find nothing.

But the challenge keeps people motivated. Finding something worth riding might take a few hour-long trips to the suburbs and an endless amount of visits to the courtyards. Or you might just get lucky.

Then one day you find it; your own un-skated splash of cement. Unfortunately you can't drag it home like a lamp.

"You have to look for certain details. And only a small number of people know what those details are."

So, you ask your buddy to hold a video camera and document you skateboarding the spot.

At least you'll have the video footage and the knowledge that you were the first one there.

The City of Children

A labyrinth of thyme, floating houses, towers stretching towards the sky, wavy islands and adventurous forests. If children could decide, the city would have no limits.

TEXT: HELLA HERNBERG • PHOTOS: NIINA HUMMELIN

At the *Arkki* children's architecture school, children learn about architecture through play. "Children don't have the same boundaries as adults. Through playful activities and fantasy games they can create lots of enchanting ideas," says Arkki's lead teacher, **Niina Hummelin**. However, activities at Arkki have become far more than just playtime. Since 2004, Arkki's students have been involved in real town planning, together with city officials and the building industry.

We are standing, looking at a large-scale clay model, a competition entry made by a group of 3-17-year-olds for *Hernesaari* (literally translating to Pea Island). This former shipyard at the shorefront of southern Helsinki will be gradually converted into a residential area after 2012. In 2006, Arkki's students were invited to create a plan that was evaluated together with other competition entries made by professional architects and a group of adult citizens. This was the first time in Finland that children had taken part in such an urban design competition.

"Children are sensitive to notice many kinds of details in the environment that adults might often miss."

In the children's vision, a large park surrounds the island. The plan shows that children yearn for a diverse streetscape with green spaces, colors and adventures.

Seven year-old **Stella** has created a "wavy" island. This is how she describes her plan: "The wavy forms and hills make the shoreline long enough for everyone. When you sail from the sea, you first see high towers reflecting the sky, and soon the smaller houses and trees appear. Simple things create the play of the island, and that is why people feel so good there."

What are the ingredients of a nice neighborhood? You need a home, a shop, a school and a bank – a village. The illustrations show 7-9-year-old children's views of a place that is good to live in.

Arkki students' models and illustrations for the urban planning project in Hernesaari.

"Concentrating on one sense at a time, like smells, sounds or touch, one can experience the environment more deeply."

In Hernesaari, children first went on an adventurous journey, climbing in high places, sniffing and sensing the atmosphere of the area.

Arkki's headmaster, architect **Pihla Meskanen**, explains the method called sensory exploration: "Concentrating on one sense at a time, like smells, sounds or touch, one can experience the environment more deeply. Sometimes we've even worked with dancers to approach space in a new way."

Even city officials have taken the children's ideas and needs seriously.

"The children's presence gave us planners a new perspective. Today there are a lot of young families who want to live in the city centre. Working with children made us realize that the whole urban environment needs to be full of discovery and inspiring places for play. It is not just a question of pointing out a few children's playgrounds here and there," explains architect

Jari Huhtaniemi from the Helsinki City Planning Department.

As children were given a chance to take part in an early phase, the process worked out well. Arkki's Hummelin recounts: "This fascinating journey taught us a lot. We noticed that if you really want results, the presence of an 'intermediary architect' is important. The children have lots of ideas but they don't speak the same language as architects. You need a person who can ensure that children will present their ideas in the right way to professionals, but who still knows how to remain objective and not lead the children in some prearranged direction."

Hummelin also noted that children are sensitive to many kinds of details in the environment that adults might often miss. In one of Arkki's earlier participatory projects in *Nupuri, Espoo*, children noticed some real flaws in the urban plan. "We went to the area in late autumn and the children found a terrain that was covered with water. There was a small stream and a bridge that was a nice spot for playing. The place had already been reserved for housing, but the children didn't think it was a smart idea as the ground was so wet. The children's observations were taken into account and in the end nothing was built on that spot."

Through their own discovery and trials, young people learn to observe the environment and critically analyze it. "Their personal relationship to the built environment develops in addition to their skills of participation," says Meskanen. She wishes to light a spark in young people's minds so that they continue to have the desire to participate in their city when they grow up, whatever their future occupation may be. ∎

3. Hidden Treasures

We set off to explore the city's emergent places and to discover tools for their creative misuse. Collective efforts are unfolding the potential in old harbors, overlooked neighborhoods and forgotten courtyards.

Kalasatama Temporary

A wide-open asphalt yard, that used to be an important Baltic cargo port, is now one of Europe's largest construction sites. During its evolution it has become a hotspot for emerging grassroots cultural activities.

TEXT: HELLA HERNBERG · PHOTOS: JOHANNES ROMPPANEN

A small skate park stands on a vacated parking lot. During the summer, men in their mid-thirties — skateboarders for life — have spent their evenings after work mixing concrete and drinking beer. At last the park seems ready for use.

By the nearby metro bridge leading to *Kulosaari* Island, construction has begun on the first blocks of a large-scale residential project. In the 2002 film by **Aki Kaurismäki**, *The Man Without a Past*, homeless people lived in a container just north of the same Kulosaari Bridge.

I am standing at the gates to *Kalasatama*, an area that used to be one of Helsinki's large cargo ports. In 2008, the harbor was moved to the eastern suburb of *Vuosaari*. As a result, wide-open asphalt fields and shorelines with new views towards downtown have opened up.

An area comprising 175 hectares will be home to about 25,000 people and 8,000 work places during the coming decades.

Architect and visual artist **Johanna Hyrkäs** has stopped by on her bike to take some photos. The city has hired her as a consultant to coordinate temporary uses and cultural activity in the empty harbor.

"Kalasatama is by far the most interesting thing in Helsinki right now. It is an honor and a privilege to be part of it."

Because of the scale of the operation in Kalasatama, construction may take almost 30 years, which has caused city officials to realize that something should be done during the time in between. Parts of the harbor have recently

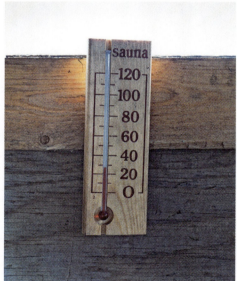

Previous page: Views to the Kruununhaka district from Ihana Café's lawn.
This page: The fences surrounding a large sand storage area were quickly turned into Helsinki's longest graffiti wall. A spontaneously built sauna has emerged at the edge of the harbor. From the port's southern tip you can see the icebreakers anchored by the Katajanokka district.

been temporarily opened to the public. The project, named "Kalasatama Temporary," aims to give the residents of Helsinki an opportunity to leave their mark on the city.

> *"The spot that once served as no more than a road sign indicating a closed port area is now a new free zone: an area for legal graffiti, art exhibitions held in a container, bicycle brunches, swimming and night movies."*

When the locks of the harbor gates were removed in 2009, it didn't take long before the first fishermen and occasional bicycle riders discovered the location. Car enthusiasts soon organized the first "American Graffiti – Drive-in Movie" show. Only a year later the place was officially introduced to the public. A new cycling route was then opened, making the harbor's seashore accessible to everyone.

During the past two years, Kalasatama has quickly evolved into a prominent stage for grassroots activities – it is now *the* place to be in Helsinki. The spot that once served as no more than a road sign indicating a closed port area is now a new free zone: an area for legal graffiti, free art exhibitions (held in a container), bicycle brunches, swimming, night movies and urban gardening.

Unknown Cargo in the Dockland

A thick green line is painted on the ground, leading the way to the harbor. We take our bikes and follow the line. The sun is high and skateboarders and graffiti painters are enjoying the August afternoon. Some boats have anchored along the shore, but the big cargo ships are gone.

We pass by the *Container Square*, where people are making preparations for the night's open-air cinema. The square consists of seven old marine containers, which the city has offered to various grassroots operators. Arranged in a circular form, they create a plaza protected from the wind: a perfect spot for punk concerts, theatre shows, poetry evenings, art exhibitions, and food events around the self-built outdoor oven, "Archie" *(see p.124)*.

One of the containers is run by *Bermuda Helsinki*. Media artist **Timo Wright**, and art pedagogist **Eeva Astala**, lend their container for free to people who want to organize non-commercial events. Their mission is to enable events that are free of charge, open for everyone, and without age limits or "other discrimination of any kind."

"I couldn't organize a heavy metal gig myself, but it's fantastic that I can do my share in making that possible, and to help people create urban culture of their own," says Astala. Wright continues: "Kalasatama is by far the most interesting thing in Helsinki right now. It is an honor and a privilege to be part of it and to see how the place will develop."

Bermuda Helsinki's experience of the summer of 2011 has been rewarding. "When you look at a crowd of people who are so excited, and watch the sun set behind the power plant, the atmosphere is so magically unique, time and again," says Wright. He is also involved with another container, *The Unknown Cargo*, which is open for unknown artists to show their works in public without hefty gallery fees.

Wright is especially proud of how well their "tenants" have behaved. "Perhaps because it is all for free, people do have respect and take it seriously. Everyone understands that the fun goes on only for as long as the place stays in nice condition."

Meals on Two Wheels

Throughout the summer of 2011, **Tuukka Ylä-Anttila** has been organizing "Bicycle Brunches" with bike repairs and food for a voluntary price. One warm day in July, the "We Love Helsinki Bicycle Day" gathered together a number of different events around the city's emerging bicycling culture and included live music on the Container Square. At night, an almost endless line of 400 cyclists went on a ride around the city, ringing their bells and winding through the streets of Helsinki. Back in Kalasatama, the night continued at *Ihana Kahvila* ("The Lovely Café") with a screening of the film *Kotipojat* ("Home Boys"), a documentary about Finnish hip-hop by **Nuutti Takkinen**.

With Johanna Hyrkäs we continue our way to Ihana. The café is at the south end of the harbor and is a

welcome oasis along the few kilometers of asphalt shoreline. The café comprises two freight containers and a recycled lawn, and it seems to be a fun and safe place for children, who play in sandpits made of concrete conduits. We sit comfortably on the green recycling bags that are filled with bubble wrap. A man is lying in a hammock reading his book. The views are great. Here you actually realize how close

Previous page: People enjoy the warm night at the We Love Helsinki Bicycle Day in July 2011.
This page: Timo Santala leads the night bicycle ride with his megaphone. Tuukka Ylä-Anttila takes on nighttime bike repairs.
Next page: The self-built skate park facing the Suvilahti power plant dressed in its winter outfit.

Kalasatama is to different parts of Helsinki: Kruununhaka, Merihaka, Katajanokka and the Korkeasaari Zoo. You can almost hear the lions roar.

Despite the great views, customers have to deviate a few kilometers from their daily routes to get there. Doesn't it seem risky to open a café in a place like this?

The owner **Sanni Jouhki** doesn't think so: "I thought this would be a small project and therefore not too risky to get started. Well, it hasn't been that small, and luckily so. There has been a really colorful crowd of customers: old and young, cyclists and construction workers, painters and even ladies from the parliament on an excursion."

Happy with this year's experience, Jouhki is intending to continue her café for the next few summers at least, as her land rent contract covers three years.

"The biggest challenge was probably during construction, when we started installing the lawn with friends. One roll weighed 1,600 kilograms and five men were not enough to move it. I would say it was harder than giving birth!"

Bureaucracy vs. Spontaneity

As we sip our ginger lemonade, Johanna Hyrkäs recalls that the first idea behind Kalasatama Temporary was based on a hunch that there were active people in Helsinki who would organize inspiring things – if they were given a little push to do so. The project was started in 2009 with an open brunch in exchange for ideas, in order to find out what people wanted to do. Later the city provided small things, such as containers, playgrounds and a water supply for urban farmers. However, for the most part, all the activity has been in people's own hands.

"Projects that we have seen this summer, like Bermuda or Ihana, show that our intuition was right. These events have really inspired

other people who are just passing by the harbor. I hope they will encourage other people to create more activity here," says the smiling architect. Yet she seems a tiny bit disappointed: "The place is so unique and full of potential, but we have only been able to realize a small percentage of the good ideas so far."

Investing in things that make people enjoy the environment is an invaluable advertisement for an area like Kalasatama that is still developing its identity. The grassroots activities have attracted great media coverage. Hyrkäs is grateful that the city has shown the courage to support a project like this. But the reality is challenging; how to apply the tactics of spontaneous, self-organized projects to the planning process of a large, bureaucratic organization that is used to making stable, long-term decisions?

Working as a consultant between the city

Above: The Bicycle Day in July 2011 ended with an open-air ride-in movie. Right: Preparations for the movie screening at Ihana Café's container.

officials and different grassroots players has had its challenges. Hyrkäs has noticed that there is a will within the city's leaders to display an image of Helsinki as a vibrant cultural city and invest in spontaneous activities, but even the best of intentions tend to get stuck somewhere in the bureaucratic machine. As the first project of its kind in Finland, Kalasatama Temporary has been a learning process. The first years have given hints as to what kind of methods and tools are needed to make the interaction between the city and its residents run more smoothly.

"What I hope to see in the future would be more courage to take risks, a clearer shared vision, and more agility to react fast in changing situations," sums up Hyrkäs. "As the time span covers a few decades, there should be room to learn from experiments and even failures."

"When you look at the crowd of people who are so excited, and watch the sun set behind the power plant, the atmosphere is so magically unique, time and again."

We decide to leave the café lawn, as the sun is scorching. Further south along the asphalt isle, there is a dubious-looking sauna, piled together from spare wood. Hyrkäs recounts how she once stayed overnight at the harbor in her caravan.

The worst graffiti gets quickly repainted in Kalasatama.

Previous page: The Hanasaari power plant towers over the construction site.

At Dodo's urban gardens people can rent their own grow bags.

"The place was really alive, even though it was a normal weekday. Graffiti painters stayed late at night, and early in the morning the first fishermen and cyclists came around."

"Only here you realize how close Kalasatama is to different parts of Helsinki: Kruununhaka, Merihaka, Katajanokka and the Korkeasaari Zoo. You can almost hear the lions roar."

We take a curve north and pass by the graffiti wall – possibly the world's longest – which hides a huge area where sand and rubble are stored during the construction works. At the east side of the harbor, facing the Korkeasaari Zoo, a large urban farm is lush and ripe for a harvest party. Someone is watering her tomatoes, and a garden gnome is standing on guard.

We stop to imagine for a moment what the place will look like in twenty years. Nobody knows yet for sure. We might be standing on the tramline leading from the Kruununhaka district towards the eastern parts of the city. If a bridge from the south is built, Kalasatama will come a great step closer to the city centre. But that is still open for debate.

What will happen here in the meantime? Well, we hope that it is up to anyone with ideas and the courage to make them reality.

↳ *www.kalasatamanvaliaika.fi*

A Pearl at the End of the Orange Line

Is it the smaller class sizes, meze tables or local voluntary activities that are making one of Helsinki's most infamous eastern suburbs look more attractive?

TEXT: TOMMI LAITIO · PHOTOS: MATTI TANSKANEN

Mellunkylä. "Where the metro does a u-turn." "Poor." "A dangerous ghetto." "The outcome of instant urbanization."

This is what most people think about Helsinki's biggest neighborhood. Statistics fan their flames. Apartments are three times cheaper than in downtown Helsinki. There are twice as many immigrants and jobless people than elsewhere. Every seventh resident is on social welfare benefits.

And the level of crime?

Phew.

Why then do people like **Jenni Keskinen** move from the city center to Mellunkylä? Keskinen is a successful, educated woman in her thirties.

"I guess it's hard to understand East Helsinki unless you grew up here," she says. "Here you can walk from your front door into the woods in five minutes. You couldn't let your dog run free downtown. And then there are the people – they are proud and uncomplicated in a good way."

"People have rolled up their sleeves and gotten down to business. Together they have decided to make the future better."

Keskinen's words resonate with experience. She is the owner of the *Helmigrilli* restaurant and she heads the entrepreneur association of the *Kontula* shopping mall, which is the heart of the neighborhood. Keskinen is one of the people who have rolled up their sleeves and gotten

down to business. Together they have decided to make the future better. Schools, the library, the pastor, town councilors and the football team have also been enlisted.

Not Without These People

The Mellunkylä activists exude charisma: No embellishments and no beating about the bush.

Take, for example, **Suvi** and **Niklas Nyström**. Producing top-quality Russian-language children's culture has required a great deal of unpaid work, tolerance for the runaround from various officials, and the payment of exorbitant rents. Their student loans evaporated into radio commercials. And still the Nyströms go on. "We couldn't have done it without these people."

Jorma Konttinen is in the same voluntary neighborhood working group as the Nyströms and Keskinen. He runs *Symppis*, a rehabilitation group for alcoholics, the homeless and mental health patients. Every day Symppis offers over three hundred people that are unable to work a place where they can be in peace. Konttinen demonstrates his sincerity by pointing out the *Mäyräbaari* drunkards' locale at the forest's edge, which can be seen from the Symppis window. He also shows the plastic crates in which the local homeless store their belongings. This too is a part of real life.

Konttinen says Mellunkylä's secret is its social carrying capacity. "As we've gotten to know each other over the years, our chemistry is in sync and there's no tension."

As proof of this, the song of a chorus of retirees can be heard through the wall. The

Symppis organization has recently talked with entrepreneurs about how cooperation could be improved. A residents' space, cultural center and a lottery stand (run by *FC Kontu*) are located in the same premises as Symppis. Could this work anywhere else in Helsinki?

Collaboration bears fruit. Jenni Keskinen says disturbances in the mall have been halved.

Good news is heard from elsewhere as well. The principal of *Vesala* High School, **Juha Juvonen**, says that, in recent years, the number of students registered at the school has increased from 250 to 365. A growing number of middle-class parents would now rather place their children in the local school than send them downtown on the metro.

Even though the school has worked hard to reduce class sizes, principal Juvonen praises the efforts of others as well: "It really started from teachers and residents noticing that the environment had been improved." As a thankyou to the community, the neighborhood newspaper is delivered into homes in students' backpacks.

The New We

Eeva-Liisa Broman, who coordinates the area's cooperation team, has an explanation for the good news. "People's lives are not about one or other service," she says. "It's about the totality.

Some of the Mellunkylä activists, from top left: Larri Helminen is the motor behind many local efforts, such as Kontu-Fest and a local newspaper. George Drayton runs the local residents' space, "Mellari." Ahmet Al-Zobeidi stands by his delicious meze table. Suvi and Niklas Nyström have fouded the multicultural children's music school, "Musikantit."

Here everyone wants to start from the ground up." According to Broman, Mellunkylä's vitality stems from a joint effort, something that has largely been lost in Helsinki. A lot can be made out of meager resources when people work together. That is, people's every day lives can be made noticeably better.

"Even though there is still much to do, the seeds of urban happiness are already germinating."

Mellunkylä. Northern Europe's biggest skateboarding hall. Nature and familiar people. Music lessons for kids and support for adults. About twenty minutes from the city center by metro. Happy student couples. **Ahmet Al Zobeid**'s bountiful *meze* table. A school zoo. *KontuFest* – the event with the most street credibility in Finland. Shops, *blinis*, asparagus, and banks at walking distance.

Even though there is still much to do, the seeds of urban happiness are already germinating. Much ground has been covered by creating a new We out of Us and Them.

↳ *www.mellunkyla.fi*

Independent Shops Make a Comeback

An excursion into Helsinki's ever-changing Kallio district discovers a new, more polished edge to the old working class neighborhood. An area that has been characterized by the bohemian air of artists, students and alcoholics is being taken over by a new generation of young families and small entrepreneurs.

TEXT: HELLA HERNBERG · PHOTOS: JOHANNES ROMPPANEN

We meet outside the *Hakaniemi* Market Hall on a gray September afternoon. Producer **Anna Pakarinen**, of the *Up With Kallio* entrepreneurs' network, walks over from the market square and says she's bought a massive pumpkin for a party that evening: "You don't have to go to a florist at all this time of year as harvest produce makes fantastic decorations!"

Urban sociologist **Pasi Mäenpää** walks down the steps of the market hall and presents us with a page ripped out of a 1987 edition of the free *City* newspaper.

The *Kallio Go!* article describes how the area was undergoing "centerfication." Traditionally a working-class neighborhood, Kallio was separated from the centre and the bourgeoisie by the *Pitkäsilta* (Long Bridge). Since the 1970's, the area has been populated by students and artists, and has gradually become a part of central Helsinki.

Large parts of Kallio's austere apartment blocks were built in the first part of the 20th century as working class housing. The high number of small apartments in the area

Siltasaarenkatu is one of Helsinki's few true city axes. What used to be perceived as "the axis from the rich to the poor" leads from downtown Helsinki up to Kallio. The church tower, designed by architect Lars Sonck, rises tall at the end of the street.

translates to a high turnover rate of residents, who live in Kallio for an average of only 3.5 years – one of the reasons why there is always something new going on.

To many, the expression "Kallio tour" (or *Kalliokierros* in Finnish) refers to bar hopping, thanks to the high frequency of cheap beer joints in the area since the economic depression of the 1990's. However, we're now setting out on a different tour of Kallio, to find out how young entrepreneurs are changing the area's image.

Prostitutes, alcoholics, the homeless, the bread line, artists, drug problems, Thai massage – these are some of the usual clichés brandished about Kallio. But the area is not really the Harlem of Helsinki. Kallio has the reputation of being an open-minded neighborhood with different nationalities, social classes and personalities coexisting side-by-side – while still being characterized by a strong "we-spirit." Heading into the 2010's, the area is polishing its edgy reputation. It is turning into a trendy middle-class district that is once again attracting families with small kids. However, its rugged history is still palpable. A romanticized working-class image still clings to Kallio and has made its way into numerous books and movies.

"Will artists soon have to move further away? Where will the next Kallio be?"

Reasonably affordable retail premises are attracting young entrepreneurs and freelancers

to the area. The new generation of entrepreneurs know their neighbors. The shops and cafés have their loyal customers, and local residents have places to hang out.

> *"The urban experience is born from pluralism."*

For these young entrepreneurs, location and atmosphere are important. Often built into the foundations of multi-storey buildings, the shops are characterized by red and white floor tiles left over from the original dairy shops that once dominated the streetscape.

Walking up the broad and ugly Siltasaarenkatu, we arrive at *Karhupuisto* (Bear Park), which was a disreputable place only 15 years ago. Since 1997, the park's patrons, the *Karhupuiston kummit*, have looked after the park together.

Led by **Saara Tolonen**, elderly "godmothers" gather to pick up cigarette butts and to tend the flowerbeds. The police big band performs at their spring flower-planting event.

Anna Pakarinen praises the spirit of co-operation in the area. The newly established *Kallio Initiative*, set up to fight general intolerance, is working on a tent village for the homeless in a nearby park in honor of the *Night of the Homeless*, which is held every October.

In fall 2011, the initiative organized its inaugural Kallio Block Party in Karhupuisto. Created as a volunteer effort, almost the only expenses for the party were permits demanded by the city. Even though making sense of various officials' permits is daunting, closing the street of *Fleminginkatu* to traffic was not too difficult. As Pakarinen points out, organizing events on a tiny budget requires extreme creativity and

Previous page: "Traditional" Kallio kiosks, beer joints and massage parlors still dominate the streetscape.
This page: The new generation of entrepreneurs is reinvigorating the area: Café Villipuutarha (left), Café Sävy and the Fem. boutique.

generous associates.

One of the new establishments is the fashionable *"Fem."* boutique, which has been run by five young designers since 2009. Their workshop is hidden behind a curtain in the store. Two baby strollers have been left outside the shop – demonstrating that even Kallio is safe these days.

At the corner of *Helsinginkatu*, the infamous breadline is open for business. **Heikki Hursti** continues the legacy of his father, **Veikko**, who started charity work decades ago. Rumors have it that the breadline will have to move to a less visible location due to opposition from a few residents.

Now that Kallio seems to be undergoing gentrification, will artists soon have to move further away? And then, where will the next Kallio be?

Pakarinen suggests *Pasila* – the old railway buildings around Helsinki's main railway junction are already being taken over by artists and urban farmers – or perhaps even the east Helsinki suburb of *Kontula,* where a new community spirit is rising *(see p.102)*.

Some people have opposed the establishment of new boutiques and companies in the area as they raise apartment prices. Mäenpää, a sociologist, is not against the neighborhood cleaning up. After all, local residents should benefit the most from the area's enhanced image. However, we all agree that the breadline should be allowed to stay where it is. The city should be a place where diverse fates can live side-by-side. The urban experience is born from pluralism.

Galleria Alkovi, a shop window with art inside, is located next to the breadline. The gallery started in 2005 and has been run by artists **Arttu Merimaa** and **Miina Hujala** for the past two years. Alkovi is like an extension of the square – exhibition openings are always held on the street. Merimaa and Hujala are interested in making the most of empty urban spaces and hope that they can bring more energy to the art scene.

The notorious *Roskapankki Square* got its nickname from a beer joint that opened during the recession of the early 1990's, but even this corner is smartening up. Some prefer to call it *Arla Square*, after *Sauna Arla*, which is one of Kallio's traditional neighborhood saunas, operating since 1929.

Kimmo Helistö, an experienced Helsinki activist and local politician, took over the sauna in spring 2007 when its previous owner retired.

"It was the first time I sat on the benches of Arla Sauna when I realized the place would die unless I started taking care of it. When the old man retired I was totally broke – maybe 40 Euros in my bank account. I just bought some beer and lemonade and thought: 'OK, let's start running a public sauna.'"

An adorable café on the corner, *Villipuutarha*, looks inviting with its decorative wallpaper, giant cinnamon rolls and stuffed moose head. For the café owner, **Katja Kannisto**, and for many of the new generation of entrepreneurs, work provides the possibility to do things they enjoy with a passion – operating profit is not necessarily their primary goal.

Moving on to Vaasankatu, we are confronted with its cluster of sex shops and their colorful ads. Towards the end of the street, the infamous *"Piritori"* (Speed Square) looks pretty calm in the daylight.

> "The Saréns did the opposite of what people usually do. They moved with a small baby from the neighboring city of Espoo to a smaller apartment in Kallio."

Our tour ends in *Café Sävy*, a cozy establishment run by the Saréns, who did the opposite of what people usually do. They moved with a small baby from the neighboring city of Espoo to a smaller apartment in Kallio.

The café has been open for less than a year and it has attracted loyal customers from the very beginning.

Kaisa Saren tells the story of an elderly gentleman that came in for his morning coffee almost every day: "He'd slap a five Euro note down and say: 'The usual, thanks.' After a few months the man didn't come in anymore. After some time, a big, scary-looking, tattooed man came in and announced that the old man, his father, had passed away." The man wanted to tell the Saréns how important the café was to his father.

A lot of elderly people live in Kallio's small apartments. One of the growing questions about the future is how will retired urbanites, who are not necessarily even that old, spend their time? Will they emerge from their homes into the city to frequent cafés or to plant flowers in the park? Or will they be institutionalized in their homes, dependent on meal delivery services? The "grannies" of Kallio are of the generation that is used to going to independent local shops.

Above: The "Roskapankki Square" or "Arla Square," with Café Villipuutarha on the right corner.
Below: Vaasankatu has an abundance of sex shops.

Previous page: The Karhupuisto park is blossoming thanks to the active grannies of the neighborhood.
This page: Typical peculiarities on the streets of Kallio.

They have seen the death of the local dairy and the rise of the new and they still meet in stocking shops to gossip.

Our tour of Kallio has provoked a great deal of questions. We ponder if the city's regulations could be made more permissive, and if officials might understand that they should encourage the actions of young entrepreneurs that promote authentic urban life.

Pakarinen hopes that, as a spokesperson for a network of small entrepreneurs, she could remind people of the "why not?" attitude.

Mäenpää continues: "Kallio has exactly what people seek in cities: atmosphere, diversity, attitude and a wide range of offerings."

"Elderly "godmothers" gather to pick up cigarette butts and to tend the flowerbeds."

In Finland, the promised land of shopping malls, the abundance of small independent shops is a relative concept. Could the little shops, cafés and creative-sector entrepreneurs of the future join forces to form a strong cluster, like the sex shops and Thai massage establishments on Vaasankatu? We shall have to wait and see.

↳ *www.upwithkallio.fi*
↳ *www.kallioliike.org*

Literary Interventions

The first Museum of the Near Future challenged local cultural expectations and brought together cultural exchange, performance, criticism and dialogue, under the guise of a book society in a vacant mansion.

TEXT AND PHOTOS: OK DO

"There are ten million stories in the Naked City. But no one can remember which one is theirs."
– LAURIE ANDERSON, 1984

The current *zeitgeist* invites artists and designers to play out new socio-politico-cultural roles in cities and communities. What enables us to operate at our most subversive is to explore and intervene in the reality of our own neighborhood, and to focus on the mundane and the close-by – while rethinking the relationships within our own society and their interaction with the rest of the world.

In the end it is the back-and-forth between bottom-up initiatives and governing structures that has the potential to make a difference. In an attempt to do just this, OK Do has set up alternative cultural institutions that serve a site-specific need.

Our project, called *Museum of the Near Future* (MNF), sets out to challenge common perceptions of what is possible and desirable between the now and the next. As an apparatus for looking sideways at institutions, cities and culture, MNF's are set up in connection with museums and other institutional contexts. They generate tension where it is needed, while providing a space for fantasies and stories.

The first MNF manifested itself as a thematic book society in Helsinki during autumn 2011. It intervened in the life of a dormant mansion in *Kaivopuisto*, one of Helsinki's oldest parks. The wooden villa that had once served as a school and was later occupied by the Museum of Finnish Architecture had been closed to the public since the 1980's. For a moment, our project turned the villa into a temporary bookshop and a place for events.

The core of "MNF I," our literary collection, was compiled by borrowing books from Helsinki libraries, downloading online texts, and by putting up a small bookshop in collaboration with a Berlin-based book distributor.

"MNF I" not only filled a gap when it came to inspiring international literature for aspiring local urbanites, but it also employed passages from written pieces in the process of reinventing the city. Different literature-related events, such as reading circles and just-in-time publishing, were organized around select books. The events sought to challenge current concepts around designing and using the city, as well as the cultural and social exchange taking place in it.

"A local chanteuse found the museum and decided to throw a spontaneous concert. Sitting on the chairs of what used to be her old school, she sang old French chansons."

A spontaneous concert by Hannele Wida, a local chanteuse and former student of the Ecole Elémentaire Francaise. Sitting on her former school stairs, Hannele was accompanied by her friend, guitarist Matti Wallenius (from the cassette player inside her bag).

One of these events took place on the maiden voyage of a future water bus line from Kaivopuisto park to nearby *Hernesaari*, a dockyard soon to be transformed into a residential area. Passengers created "water bus poems," reinterpreting French poet **Jacques Jouet**'s *Poèmes de métro* (subway poetry), in order to see further into the future of the area.

In the course of our miniature public forums unexpected encounters occurred. A local chanteuse, **Hannele Wida**, found the museum and decided to throw a spontaneous concert. Sitting on the chairs of what used to be her old school, Hannele sang old French chansons accompanied by her friend, guitarist **Matti Wallenius** (from the tape player inside her bag).

"Since Helsinki, with its emerging future areas, has the potential to become almost anything, we should take time to dream up and debate what would make it the best place on earth."

Before opening its doors as an office and exhibition space for the Museum of Finnish Architecture in 1957, the Kaivopuisto villa by Carl Henrik Nummelin (1881) served as a home for a lithographic atelier and two international schools, Svenska Samskolan and Ecole Elémentaire Française. Since the 1980's, when the museum activities moved to a new location on Kasarmikatu, the building has been closed to the public. Photo: Hella Herberg

With these literary interventions, "MNF I" took its own position on ongoing micro-political participation in Helsinki. More than defining a specific "what," it focused on the "how," offering tools for imagining, discussing and working towards an ideal city from many perspectives.

Embedded in the process was the idea that since Helsinki, with its emerging future areas, has the potential to become almost anything, we should take time to both dream up and debate what would make it the best place on earth. Perhaps it is just these sorts of experimental initiatives that actually light up authentic reformation in cities and institutions.

We believe the reformation of a city can start from small initiatives, where imagination and close collaboration override more conventional strategies and means.

Selected sources:

Jouet, Jacques (2000). *Poèmes de métro.* Paris: P.O.L.

Latour, Bruno (2008). *What is the Style of Matters of Concern? Two Lectures in Empirical Philosophy.* Assen: Van Gorcum

Puolakka, Anni & Sutela, Jenna (ed) (2012). *Museum of the Near Future I.* Helsinki: OK Do.

The City of Matters of Concern reading circle explored what it means to care for a city, drawing from (or bastardizing) sociologist Bruno Latour's notions. Another, The Climate of Public Space, looked at different ways of leading public life inside in a city of long winters and cold, dark agoras.

Opening Doors to Helsinki's Hidden Places

OpenHouseHelsinki provides Helsinki citizens and visitors with tours that discover the city's secrets.

TEXT: MERI LOUEKARI

Underground, over roofs, in secret gardens, on private islands. In the mosque, on an icebreaker, in the home of a legendary designer. OpenHouseHelsinki opens doors to places where ordinary people usually have no access.

Open House is a concept spreading as a worldwide network. After its start in London 1992, doors have been opened to new places in cities around the world, including New York, Melbourne, Barcelona and Jerusalem. The Helsinki event, run by the Finnish Association of Architects, reached its current scope in 2007. Smaller events, which covered only a few locations, have been held since 2001.

Cities around the world are competing on attractiveness. Architecture, urban events and a unique sense of place have become the success factors of today. Even though Helsinki is well known for its high quality architecture and the character of its urban environment, many of the city's most interesting places are closed to the general public.

To cover this gap OpenHouseHelsinki organizes guided tours, led by professional architects and designers, to interesting interiors, closed industrial areas, hidden courtyards, and to both old and new architectural jewels. Moreover, the event offers exhibitions, lectures and workshops for the whole family. Open House aims to bring professionals and the public closer together, and to open up discussion and interaction.

"The tours have led visitors down into the sewer network, through the locked gates of shipyards, and to coffee tastings in roasteries."

Above: At the Open House 2010 six lucky people won tickets to an underground world tour. Photo: Hertta Ahvenainen

Below: The Wärtsilä dockyard in Hietalahti was strictly gated for over 100 years. First opened by the Open House in 2009, it will soon be transformed into a housing and business area. Photo: Hella Hernberg

How the city works is one of the themes that has particularly piqued people's interest. These tours have led visitors down into the sewer network, through the locked gates of shipyards, and to coffee tastings in roasteries.

There are also numerous islands just off the coast of Helsinki Peninsula, which few get a chance to visit. OpenHouseHelsinki has taken visitors by boat to the closed military islands of *Santahamina* and *Lonna*, as well as to the artists' island of *Harakka*.

Icebreakers keep Helsinki harbor areas open during the winter. Two of them opened for Open House 2011.
Photo: Johanna Bruun

Hundreds of people followed architect Juha Ilonen on a tour through closed courtyards. Photo: Johanna Strandman

At best the locations inspire discussion or evoke memories. The tours to churches and mosques have led to contemplations on what makes a place sacred and what are various religions' holiest places in Helsinki. In the *Garden of Dreams* workshop, children built the best garden in the world from pipe cleaners, tissue paper and modeling clay. Using open source principles, the *Post Office of the Future* collected people's greetings onto postcards, which were turned into an installation in the attic of an empty port warehouse. The messages will be delivered in the 2020's to the future residents of *Jätkäsaari*, when the neighborhood that is currently under construction has been completed.

The tours that opened the gates of the closed backyards of urban blocks of *Punavuori* and *Kruununhaka* raised people's curiosity. A lady that took part in one of the tours reminisced about a courtyard in *Töölö* where she and her friends used to pinch apples as children. The lady hoped to be able to revisit one day to revive those memories.

Growing interest from visitors and the media provides proof that people are keen to know more about their built environment. Actions that open communications and build trust, in direct interaction between professional planners and the public, are key to fostering better knowledge and appreciation of architecture.

↳ *www.openhousehelsinki.fi*

4. Actions for Real Food

An appreciation of good food is exploding and Helsinki is becoming a truly intriguing food city. Ingenuity is flourishing in informal restaurants and urban farms, and fine dining is traveling towards previously undreamed locations.

The Quest for Bread

*What to do when you can't find a bakery selling fresh bread?
Bake your own? Or build your own oven on a forgotten asphalt yard?*

TEXT AND PHOTOS: KATHARINA MOEBUS

When I moved to Finland in 2008, I soon wondered about the lack of bakeries. Having grown up in Germany, I had simply taken for granted that there were small bakeries selling fresh bread around every corner. With roots in both countries (a father from Bremen, Germany, and a mother from Rovaniemi, Finland), I had warm childhood memories of long Sunday breakfasts with fresh *Sonntagsbrötchen* and feasts of traditional Finnish *rieska* flatbread during our Lapland visits on Easter holidays.

In my quest for freshly baked bread, I started growing my own sourdough starter. After some half-successful fights with my gas oven, I suddenly found myself passionately baking fresh buns and sourdough bread loaves on a regular basis.

I found library books describing the Finns' passion for rye bread, and was surprised at the variety of bread types that are typical of the country's different regions. Bread is, as in any other country, of great importance here.

Perhaps it was not the Finns' laziness that caused the lack of bakeries in cities after all. The fact that urbanism has grown so late and quickly in this country might explain, to some extent, the smaller amount of cafés and bakeries compared to Central Europe and, of course, the general tendency towards big supermarkets replacing these local services in many countries.

"Leipä miehen tiellä pitää."

(Good bread keeps a man on the road.)
Finnish sayings about bread often have a double meaning, referring to both bread and livelihood.

The crew for building Helsinki's first public outdoor oven was recruited through different Internet channels. Photo: Joel Rosenberg

Sayings and phrases, such as "our daily bread" or "got some dough?" reveal that bread is a metaphor for money and food. They also reflect how a country's population works, lives and thinks, what kind of climate is prevalent, and how things are produced. Bread makes it possible to raise a discussion while people get together around a shared table.

Being an artist of a sort, I wondered how I could use bread as a material for my work, and promote and reawaken urban and traditional bread culture in Helsinki. Another Nordic tradition also became of interest: *talkoot*, which translates from Finnish as "community effort." People who barely know each other, traditionally neighbors in the countryside, get together and help build something like a barn, a sauna, or an oven – out of nothing. Thanks to social media, this tradition has been revived in Finnish cities, even if the city might often be the place where gratuitous anonymity and notorious selfishness prevail.

In 2010 I was planning my final thesis at Aalto School of Art & Design. Lost traditions and rituals, old knowledge and artisan skills, new ways of learning (internet tutorials), sharing (open source), and doing together (talkoot, forums and Facebook events), became central themes in my work. I decided to organize a series of food events as metaphors for different food production steps: *Fertilize, grow, prepare, consume, and salvage*. These were summed up in the project's smashing title "5 - The dish."

The idea of building a public outdoor oven came into being, as I wanted to take bread-

At the inauguration event for the oven, people baked their own flatbreads with recipes sourced from grandmothers, websites, and their own imagination.

making further from my own kitchen and turn it into a communal activity. Through an Internet community called Public School, I was quickly connected with a lady who had a similar dream. **Salla Kuuluvainen**, a food activist from Helsinki, brought a friend, **Tanja Korvenmaa**, to our first meeting. Together we arranged a workshop for building a cob oven, a type of furnace that can be easily built from natural materials. *Kalasatama*, the former cargo port, was a perfect spot for us, as it had just been opened up as a testing ground for grassroots activities *(see p.90)*.

"Leipänsä edestä koirakin haukkuu."

(Even a dog barks for his bread.)

Answers from professional furnace builders had been doubtful; who could build a functioning oven without professionals!? Undeterred we decided to trust Internet tutorials. We gathered together a group of international people – of all ages and backgrounds – who had all met through the Internet. I was amazed with the ease of the process. All materials were retrieved from the nearby environment – recycled from construction sites or taken straight from nature. Only the baking surface stones, bought from the hardware store, cost us around 60 Euros.

The oven also got a name, "Archie." Before taking him into use, we went to learn baking at *Avikainen*, one of the remaining traditional family bakeries in *Kallio*, Helsinki. A group of students learnt how to bake the infamous Finnish *reikäleipä*, a rye bread made from sourdough

Preparation for the first events of "5 - The Dish." Before taking the open-air oven into use, people learnt how to bake traditional rye bread at Kallio's Avikainen bakery. At the oven's inauguration in Kalasatama, participants could stamp their flatbreads with different words.

Communal stew at the "Prepare" event at the outdoor museum on Seurasaari island.

with a hole in the middle. Traditionally the bread is stuck on a rod and hung in the ceiling to be dried and stored safe from mice.

"Kenen leipää syöt, sen lauluja laulat."

(Whose bread you eat, his tune you'll sing.)

And so the time came for Archie's inauguration. On a fall Sunday afternoon at Kalasatama's Container Square, we got together to bake rieska. People were asked to bring a recipe of their choice, and soon flatbreads of different sizes and shapes came out of the oven. Eating a warm self-made piece of bread from a self-built oven with melting butter, outdoors in the middle of Finland's capital, felt quite magical.

Later, on a crisp September evening, people were invited to join an open-air one-pot dinner on *Seurasaari* Island, a park and outdoor museum of traditional Finnish houses and barns. People brought a raw ingredient of their choice and a hearty stew was prepared by the open campfire. Everybody gathered around the fire to warm their hands and spirits while the stew was cooking. In the local tradition, the bread offered was *piimälimppu*, typical of the *Uusimaa* region.

The project concluded with a taste of bread from the other end of the food chain. It is hard to estimate how much food is actually discarded during production, transport, selling and consumption. Recent studies estimate that about one third of global food production is lost or wasted each year.[1] This final event was held in my kitchen, the same place I had made my

The fifth and final event, "Salvage," turned supermarket waste bread into traditional German Knödels.

first sourdough experiments. A huge bag of old bread, salvaged from the supermarket trash, was turned into *Knödels*, a traditional German recipe for reusing stale bread. The Finnish guests seemed to enjoy tasting those quite suspicious-looking slimy bread balls for the first time.

"Toisen kuolema toisen leipä."

(One man's death is another man's bread.)

During the time we got together to build, cook and bake, a growing network of people from different backgrounds came into being. For me, this was the most rewarding outcome of the project. I do have very positive hopes for the future of self-organized grassroots movements, even in cities. Communication technology makes sharing ideas and planning activities possible, and the necessary philosophy seems to be in the air as the common *zeitgeist*.

The world is shrinking through its interconnectedness, and it is up to people to make it an even better place. Even if it is just by creating a few blissful smiles with the scent of freshly baked buns coming straight from the homemade oven.

---

1 Gustavson, Jenny; Cederberg, Christel; Sonesson, Ulf; van Otterdijk, Robert; Meybeck, Alexandre (2011). *Global Food Losses and Food Waste. Extent, Causes and Prevention.* Rome: FAO.
www.mtt.fi/english/foodspill

See also:

Fuad-Luke, Alasdair (2009). *Design Activism. Beautiful Strangeness For A Sustainable World.* London: Earthscan.

Rauramo Ulla (2004). *Ruis. Suomalaisten salainen ase.* Jyväskylä: Atena Kustannus Oy.

Vogelzang, Marije (2010). *Eat Love. Food Concepts by Eating Designer Marije Vogelzang.* Amsterdam: BIS Publishers.

Notes From an Urban Farmer

In Helsinki and other cities small guerrilla farms are taking over unused plots of land, bringing a green glow and renewed purpose to forgotten and unexpected corners of the concrete jungle.

TEXT AND PHOTOS: HELLA HERNBERG

During the month of August 2011, as summer fades, I have been troubled by unusual dilemmas: Can you have too much fresh coriander? How much rocket can a person eat in one day? I have been improvising in my kitchen with variations of *tabbouleh* and *pesto*, and I have manipulated zucchini into previously unimaginable forms. On workdays I am often found, like a campfire nursery rhyme, carrying bucketloads of water out of my workspace window to our exposed terrace.

In May 2011, my colleagues and I planted an urban bag farm on a 120 meter-long terrace – formerly the old loading dock of the derelict harbor warehouse that is now home to our workspaces. The warehouse is in *Jätkäsaari* (which literally translates to "Lumberjack Island") at the heart of a vast building site that is destined to become part of a new inner-city district. The dock is perhaps a little too windy for gardening, but the views are more than adequate compensation. While tending the zucchini, we can see the towering cranes of the *Hernesaari* shipyard skyline across the water. Occasionally we become distracted as an old *barque* floats by.

"Who could think of a less provocative action than growing vegetables?"

The day we built our garden was exhilarating. In the morning, a truck drove to our front yard (which had been masquerading as a road construction site for some time) and poured eight cubic meters of black soil up against our threshold. We furnished ourselves with buckets and gloves and began toiling, filling our grey garden sacks with soil.

For several months we had been preparing our plan of action. We reached agreement with the local water management company to deliver compost filtered from sewage water free of charge, and we placed an order for industrial cement bags suitable for farming. Recycled Swiss carry bags had also arrived, scraped together from a relative's workplace. Having noted that each bag would weigh almost 1,000 kilograms, we also had the foresight to procure a pump cart and freight elevator for relocating the farm bags to the second floor terrace. After a great deal of hard work we were able to plant the first seeds.

Dodo's Guerrillas

For inspiration and know-how about urban farming, we have to thank the people of the Dodo NGO, who recently nurtured a boom in urban farming in Helsinki.

In 2009 news spread about a vegetable plantation in the unused rail yards of Pasila, adjacent to Finland's main national rail artery. Activists from Dodo had been inspired by examples of guerrilla gardening from around the world and were cultivating the idea in Helsinki.

Päivi Raivio from Dodo describes how their first garden was organized: "We scraped together old wooden pallets under snow and built our first grow bins. Our theme for the year 2009 was food and we wanted to demonstrate how to grow clean and local vegetables in an urban environment. Almost all of us were inexperienced in farming – our point was to show that it's not rocket science. The first crop of vegetables turned out much better than anticipated. There was actually too much food for the people involved, so it was shared around in urban festivals."

Coinciding with the growing discussion about climate change, Dodo's first urban farming project was a hot topic in Helsinki, embraced by the media and awarded for its sustainable achievements. Even the unauthorized use of hidden wasteland in Pasila did not bother anyone.

"Who could think of a less provocative action than growing vegetables?" added Päivi Raivio.

One of the key questions asked about urban farming is whether food grown in the city is clean and safe to eat. "To prove this, our vegetables from 2009 were tested in *MetropoliLab* with clean results," Päivi recounts. "Still, salads and other leafy vegetables should always be rinsed before eating. The most important thing to note is that the soil must be clean; that's why it's best to use separate containers that don't touch the ground directly, as it might be polluted."

Dodo has come up with several innovative solutions for this: bins built of scrap wood, bags, a 1950's Vespa and abandoned shopping trolleys. Even car tires can be piled together for growing potatoes.

Since 2009, the number of urban farmers in Helsinki has been growing. Dodo's gardens have expanded to different districts in Helsinki,

including *Vallila*, where neighbors spotted an empty lot and now run a garden together with children from the nearby day-care center.

Dodo has also tested urban apiculture and created an accessible courtyard-farming concept for urban housing blocks.

For the summer of 2012, Päivi Raivio has plans with a small group of activists for a new kind of test laboratory for urban agriculture, making use of an old rail turntable in Pasila. "We hope to grow rare plants – almost extinct traditional species – that people could get to know better. There will also be a café and different events throughout the year."

Your Own Personal Farmer?

If you really want to feed your family, a few square meters of land in a bag may not be enough. In the eastern Helsinki district of *Herttoniemi*, a collective of people have been busy running their own field.

The summer of 2011 has seen the first experiment of its kind in Helsinki based on a model called Community Supported Agriculture (CSA). Food activist **Salla Kuuluvainen**, and **Olli Repo**, who runs a local food circle in Herttoniemi, decided to start a food cooperative together in March 2011, and found 115 members to join them. Each member has to invest a small amount of money – a few hundred Euros – for each growing season. With these funds the cooperative has rented a field of 1.3 hectares in the neighboring town of Vantaa and hired a "personal farmer" – a gardener who takes care of the main duties in the field. The harvest is coordinated via online message boards and shared equally. Each week the group can collect their share from a garage in Herttoniemi.

"People have been very devoted and enthusiastic, and we also do a lot of community work in the field, especially during the harvest.

Previous page: Putting together the terrace farm in Jätkäsaari in May 2011. The soil delivery arrives on the front yard (a road construction site) and the workspace members shovel soil into grow bags with plastic baskets. (Photos bottom and right: Katja Hagelstam.) Above: The first marigolds on the terrace facing the Hernesaari dockyard. In addition to the grey cement bags and recycled carry bags, the classic blue Ikea bags proved useful for farming – though not very long-lasting.

Cress, coriander, radish and fava beans were among the successful plants at the Jätkäsaari terrace farm. The nutritious soil – composted from sewage water – worked best with leafy greens and zucchinis, but it turned out that most root vegetables needed a different kind of growing environment.
Next page: The Dodo NGO's vegetable farm at the Pasila railyard pioneered Helsinki guerrilla gardening. This construction on top of a 1950's Vespa is one of Dodo's many gardening inventions. Photo: Kirmo Kivelä / Dodo.

The best thing about a communal field is that consumers get to know more about where and how their food is grown, and also farmers get to know their clients. Solidarity is important both ways," says Kuuluvainen.

"The act of following something growing from a tiny seed, and witnessing its transformation into an edible plant, is a stirring and moving experience for a city dweller."

The first field experiment was not without its challenges. Kuuluvainen points out: "Our first problem was that it was difficult to find a field, and we got started a bit late in the spring. The field wasn't in very good condition, and that's why this year's crop turned out rather small. For next year we've found a new field, where we'll have a ten-year contract. We'll probably also recruit more members as there has been growing interest. But despite the little challenges, people's enthusiastic spirit and positive feedback have been really encouraging."

From Mesopotamia to Helsinki

Farming in an urban context is not a recent invention. Its roots go back to the ancient cities of the Middle East, where people grew vegetables in their household gardens. During the World Wars city farms were important to secure people's nourishment. Rabbits were grown on London balconies and the *Tiergarten* park in Berlin was harnessed for farming.

Even today, we are not speaking about a marginal phenomenon. Berlin has over 2000 communal gardens. It is estimated that 15 to 20 percent of the world's food is grown in cities,

Happy amateur farmers harvesting mint, beetroot and turnips in Jätkäsaari, October 2011.

much of it in developing countries. In Shanghai, 60% of vegetables, 100% of milk and 90 % of eggs are produced in the city area.[1]

Helsinki has a long tradition of growing household vegetables. The municipal allotment gardens, which often host tiny garden cottages, are currently highly sought after with prices rising every year.

Luckily it is not that difficult to find places for smaller urban farms outside traditional gardening locations. Compared to an allotment garden, a few bags or boxes of soil may be a much more relaxed alternative for someone who doesn't want to devote themselves entirely to tending land. Small tasks, like watering, are easily shared with friends. Many of the usual plagues on gardens, such as weeds or city bunnies, are much less likely to cause a nuisance in a bag farm on tarmac. We have observed that, on our second floor terrace garden by the harbor, there is very little other flora or fauna around to disturb the zucchini.

Consumer and Community

During fall 2011 in Jätkäsaari, we have had the pleasure of decorating our salads with crisp cress flowers, similar to those I remember from childhood. We are still anticipating how the first soup of self-grown Jerusalem artichokes will turn out, but our carrot greens have already proved to be useful ingredients. Next year we are considering moving our garden to the roof, if we can come up with a viable solution to deliver the water supply.

Being able to discover an abandoned location in the city and growing food there is a great experience in many ways. The most alluring aspect of urban farming might not

Due to the warm autumn and late winter in 2011, the Jätkäsaari farm blossomed in November – a rare phenomenon at Helsinki latitudes.

even be the food itself. Just the act of following something growing from a tiny seed, and witnessing its transformation into an edible plant, is a stirring and moving experience for a city dweller.

> "People start looking at their city with new eyes. Why is that lot standing empty? Growing one's own food mixes the roles of consumer and producer and increases people's awareness."

Urban farming highlights our fascination and concern for food's origins, and our yearning to socialize. Food brings people together, and not just for eating. It turns out that the solution to having too much fresh coriander and salad is simple: invite friends over for a harvest party.

Päivi Raivio sums up the positive dimensions of urban agriculture: "Farming is a way to influence one's environment in a concrete way. People start looking at their city with new eyes. Why is that lot standing empty? Farming creates new communities, which again create more activities that make people happy, like harvest parties. Growing one's own food mixes the roles of consumer and producer and increases people's awareness. After all, plants are also aesthetic. More green hues against these asphalt yards cannot be such a bad thing."

↳ www.kaupunkiviljely.fi

---

1 Vijoen, Andre (ed.) (2005). *Continuous Productive Urban Landscapes. Designing Urban Agriculture for Sustainable Cities.* Oxford: Architectural Press.

See also:

Reynols, Richard (2008). *On Guerrilla Gardening: A Handbook for Gardening without Boundaries.* London: Bloomsbury.

The Day of Independent Restaurateurs

On Restaurant Days anyone can open up informal cafés, fine-dining restaurants and bicycle bars. The event, created by a group of friends in spring 2011, is already becoming an international festival.

TEXT: IDA KUKKAPURO

Two hundred new restaurants! Two hundred!

Thanks to the idea of a group of friends, a spontaneous celebration of food culture named Restaurant Day (Ravintolapäivä in Finnish), was born in May 2011. For its second incarnation the following August, the number of pop-up restaurants in Helsinki grew exponentially. For one day the city offered bone marrow toast, chocolate-coated bacon, Japanese omelet, Basque *pintxos*, raw food and frogs' legs. All kinds of delicacies that many would like to enjoy but are impossible to find on the Helsinki high street.

The idea has channeled criticism of Finland's strict food control and restaurant licensing into the form of a carnival. **Olli Sirén**, one of the founders of Restaurant Day, is pleased with the event's massive popularity. "People want to party, not rebel. Then again, partying doesn't preclude rebelling. People are sharing what makes them feel good. That's why we chose to

Above: Borscht soup at *Kuchnia Polska*.
Next page: In August, there were several restaurants and cafes in Karhupuisto Park, Kallio. *Blin Na Ya* served blinis and salad. Photos: Veikko Kähkönen

focus on having fun – instead of highlighting the protest aspect of the event."

The restaurants that open up during Restaurant Day can be run by anyone. Eateries open in homes, on street corners and in parks. Dining spots are marked onto Google Maps and word spreads via Facebook. "Food is an easy theme but the success of Restaurant Day

Above: *Le Frog* brought frog's legs to Helsinki's waterfront for a day. Below: *Kolme luukkua* (Three Shutters) in Kruununhaka served starters, main courses and desserts out of three adjacent windows. Next page: *Alppikadun voileivät* sold sandwiches from a third floor apartment window. Photos: Tuomas Sarparanta. The following spread: *Kuchnia Polska* served the best of Polish cuisine in the largest courtyard in Scandinavia. Photo: Veikko Kähkönen.

isn't all about food. This is a brilliant example of how social media sharing permeates into reality. Restaurant Day is an event that allows grown-ups to play."

Sirén thinks that the first Restaurant Day's *Alppikadun voileivät* window kiosk nicely characterizes the nature of the event: **Mikko Kjellberg** and **Penny Nymark**'s kiosk was set up in a third floor apartment and sandwiches were lowered to people at street level in a basket.

The first event in May 2011 was featured in the evening news on every Finnish channel. Restaurant Day was timed perfectly. In the spring, petitions had been signed on behalf of the *Maunulan maja* ski café's fresh donuts, and beach café *Tyyni* by Töölö bay. The Maunula café's permit was revoked because its exhaust ducting was not the right shape. Meanwhile, one single pedestrian, who had tripped on a hose that ran across the pavement, had complained about café Tyyni and it was shut down. But thanks to the actions of thoughtful citizens, both cafés were later allowed to resume service.

The sale of food is meticulously supervised in Finland, but setting up a restaurant for one day is permitted. Selling alcohol without a license however, is forbidden. After the August restaurant day, the National Supervisory Authority for Welfare and Health was concerned because the police did not react to the illegal sale of alcohol.

Sirén says: "The first two events were systematically unsupervised. Thus the bicycle wine bar, as well as the pintxo restaurant and microbrewery, were able to operate without incident." However, in November, when the third Restaurant Day was appearing, police took the event under closer supervision.

The organizers of Restaurant Day have since established an official association. However, the responsibility for food safety remains with the one-day restaurateurs.

Sirén thinks hygiene concerns are unwarranted: "The risks are no greater than in ordinary food stores or when visiting friends. Social pressure keeps the individual pop-up operators in check. No one wants to serve bad food in his own restaurant. The risks are bigger in industrial production, where responsibility is faceless."

In future, the plan is to organize Restaurant Day four times a year. At the November 2011 edition, most restaurants were expected to stay indoors because of the weather – but with Nordic creativity, many outdoor stands were opened amongst the 300 new pop-up establishments.

The *B-smokery* prepared heavy portions of meat by the sea, while the *Puu-Vallilan Puuro ja Pakuri* offered a variety of porridges and

Ravintola kääntöpöytä (Restaurant Turntable) offered urban farming delicacies at the old rail yard in Pasila. Photo: Timo Santala. In *Apaja* (Fishing Ground) every portion was a surprise. Photo: Veikko Kähkönen *Le Garage* served oxtail soup and maki rolls. Photo: Heidi Uutela. *16 mm* presented 16 mm films and served hot dogs with 16 cm long Frankfurters. Photo: Veikko Kähkönen

Left: *Raamenya* served ninja food in the night time. Photo: Timo Santala. Right: In *Yösnägäri Kakkonen* (Night Grill Number Two) the cassette DJ entertained the audience and fights were strictly forbidden. Photo: Tuomas Sarparanta

hot *chaga* tea on a straw-covered table in the wooden Vallila district.

"The event was systematically unsupervised. Thus the bicycle wine bar, as well as the pintxo restaurant and microbrewery, were able to operate without incident."

Restaurant Day has received widespread media recognition and awards. In December 2011, the event was granted the annual Finland Award, chosen by our 35-year-old Minister for Culture and his team.

When asked to define the wildest scenario for Restaurant Day in 2022, Sirén pauses to think. "Could it happen in 2015 already? That's when Restaurant Day will have become an international festival that is celebrated four times a year. Maybe not in North Korea but in all civil societies."

About 40 establishments were opened for the first Restaurant Day, about 200 for the second and 300 for the third. By February 2011, the event had already spread from Europe to South Korea, Thailand, Japan and Nicaragua. With the same rate of growth, by the end of 2013 there might be so many restaurants that the figure will not even fit on the screen of a pocket calculator.

↪ *www.restaurantday.org*

Is It Safe To Eat These?

Urban foraging rides show 21st century Helsinkians where to find hidden fruit and berry troves.

TEXT: JOEL ROSENBERG · PHOTOS: JOHANNES ROMPPANEN

It's in our genes. We feel its draw as summer fades into fall. Gathering is the oldest profession of humankind.

For the past three years we've come together for an end-of-summer ritual. We pump up our bike tires and ride to modern tussocks on urban foraging rides to hunt for the bounty on offer in Helsinki's parks and wastelands.

Urban nature is ripe for harvesting. On our shared trips even born-and-bred Helsinkians find themselves turned into tourists in their own neighborhoods: "I go by here every day but I've never noticed this pear tree!" There are about ten stops — harvesting spots — along the two-to-three hour route.

The locations of berry and mushroom spots used to be passed down through generations by word-of-mouth. Shared forays into nature used to teach people from a very early age where the best picking spots were and which species were edible. This transfer of knowledge is a dying tradition, especially in cities. Not everyone has close relatives in the countryside or a grandma at the cottage. Foraging rides are an attempt to fill this information and skills gap in a 21st century urban context.

"Shared forays into nature used to teach people from a very early age where the best picking spots were and which species were edible."

Urban foraging rides stem from a basic need: people want to be in touch with their surroundings and to submit to nature for sustenance. Foraging, the group, discovery

September 2011, 1 km from downtown Helsinki: Sea buckthorns and chokeberries (previous page), pine nuts, Japanese quinces and apples were found on the route of the year's first Urban Foraging Ride.

"This transfer of knowledge is a dying tradition, especially in cities. Foraging rides are an attempt to fill this information and skills gap in a 21st century urban context."

and natural rhythms are eternal qualities of our being. Memories are born when foraging in groups. A life path attaches to previously meaningless places and fellow travelers. Helsinki is a better place to live in when its fabric is laced with the positive experiencs of encounters with other urbanites and with nature.

An excerpt from my foraging diary:

> "I have to slow down near the Winter Garden. Little yellow suns glow in the bushes between the bike path and the lakeside walking trail: Japanese Quinces. I reach my hand through thorny branches and pick one. It has a perfumy scent. The aroma does not transport me to another reality or memories of summer – it's one of the scents of fall in Helsinki – it's easy to pass but still it belongs here."

Naturally, in addition to feeling good and exercise, we find something to harvest: apple trees reminiscent of old manors, nut bushes planted by squirrels, chokeberry bushes planted by the parks department, plums, rose hips. Tips for making preserves are shared and experiences are compared, but most of all everything is sampled. Two questions are asked during every foraging ride: "Can I pick these?" and "Is it safe to eat these?"

The Nordic countries' liberal everyman's rights applies to the cities too. Parks are public spaces and prohibition signs have not been posted. An urban forager's harvest is safe to eat after a good rinse.

There are many types of forager. The rides often include children with their parents. Some are along for the entire route, some only for a few stops. It's important to be in a group, so you don't have to draw the attention of passers-by on your own. When foraging in a group, we are all "everymen" to whom I hope passers-by will relate. Group berry picking is a participatory activity that requires many of the senses; it is a tonic for the experiences of alienation and loneliness that plague modern society.

↪ *www.satokartta.net*

Cooking Under the Sun

At the Solar Kitchen Restaurant, experimental lunches are cooked with solar energy. Solar-powered cooking is possible at Nordic latitudes, but only when the sun shines.

TEXT: HELLA HERNBERG · PHOTOS: JOHANNES ROMPPANEN

It's getting cloudy. On any other day this wouldn't be worth mentioning, but we are heading to test the temporary *Solar Kitchen Restaurant* in Kalasatama. The revolutionary concept by Catalan designer **Martí Guixe**, and Finnish chef **Antto Melasniemi**, serves food that is prepared using only solar energy, with parabolic cookers that look like TV antennas.

Surrounded by asphalt, there is a large white square painted on the ground, where wooden tables and parabolic solar cookers are arranged. The tables are almost full, but we manage to squeeze in.

The solar cooker is traditionally used for cooking in countries with scarce energy resources, as an environmentally friendly option for making food without using wood, but it has rarely been harnessed for fine dining experiments. At first, the idea of using this system in the north, at 60 degrees latitude, seems strange. However, having traveled from the Milan Design Fair, via the Midnight Sun Film Festival in Lapland, and finally on to Helsinki, the chef convinces us that the Nordic sun should be adequate to heat the pans up to 300°C. That is, if it is a sunny day.

"The whole experience is different when you're at the mercy of the weather and you can't plan everything beforehand. It's an ongoing learning process."

Actions for Real Food   153

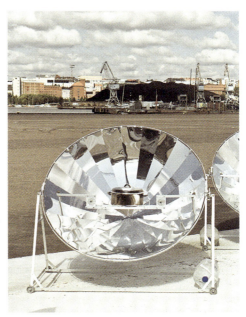

The chef, Antto Melasiemi, prepares chocolate mousse cake and bean stew at the Solar Kitchen Restaurant in Kalasatama. Next page: The "restaurant space" was a large white square painted on asphalt.

For Guixe and Melasniemi, two visionaries that both have a history of experimenting with food, solar cooking means a whole new way of approaching a restaurant. The parabolic cooker affects the texture and taste of the food in a different way from conventional cooking because the heat radiates three-dimensionally from all angles. "The whole experience is different when you're at the mercy of the weather and you can't plan everything beforehand. It's an ongoing learning process," explains Melasniemi.

Our starter salad is a hearty mix of seasonal vegetables and wild herbs. The chef explains that today's dish is a bit too acidic because the sun went hiding during cooking and the taste didn't have time to develop correctly. For the main course a little more heat wouldn't have done any harm, but it still has a rich taste. My companion's favorite dish is the dessert: a chocolate mousse cake with blueberries, gooseberries and caramel sauce.

As soon as we finish the 3-course lunch,

the first raindrops fall. Staff start dragging tablecloths away, a man runs holding a cardboard beer box as a makeshift rain cover, and the waitresses turn black garbage bags into raincoats. *"Mañana, vacación,"* someone says. "Tomorrow, restaurant closed."

This is the Finnish summer. ■

5. Slow vs. Grow

Helsinki is growing fast, but slower lifestyles are booming. New, joyful and green ideas are challenging our conventions about urban wellbeing and illuminating the possibilities for a more sustainable future.

A Tale of Two Hearts

A generation from now, will Helsinki and Tallinn be connected as a twin city filled with local urbane industries — with small factories, craft workshops, courtyard cafes and scientific research labs flourishing side by side in the heart of the city?

TEXT: BRYAN BOYER · ILLUSTRATION: PENT TALVET

As soon as she glances at the teacup rattling in its saucer, the jostling stops. "Eighteen minutes left," Anna says to her seatmate. The rail tunnel between Helsinki and Tallinn — the longest in the world — is also its largest timepiece. It tells one time only, but does it precisely. Eighteen minutes before coming to a careful stop at Helsinki's *Hernesaari* station the train passes over a small dimple in the tracks that sets things jittering about, as if to let you know there's still time for another cup of tea. It's the kind of quirk that inevitably comes from making real things. Anna appreciates this as she can share the same charms with customers who seek out the bikes built in her courtyard factory in downtown Helsinki.

The train comes to a stop beneath a station built as a careful snowflake of timber and glass. Ghanaian and Chinese tourists are snapping pictures of this curious crystal, as they always do, while daily commuters drowsily sip flat whites and cinnamon rolls at the station's reputable cafes.

"Many of the district's courtyards have been converted into thriving pockets of activity including communal gardens, micro industrial parks, and restaurants."

Slow vs. Grow 159

Built in the 2020's, during a time of careful but daring investment, the connection between Tallinn and Helsinki is now the crown jewel of the Baltic Ring Rail. Many were skeptical about the project, but with some hindsight it was an infrastructural gambit that has breathed a new spirit into the pair of sleeper capitals. It was sold as a mere "link" between the two cities but instead it has proven to be more substantial. Essential, even. At a moment when global cities were fighting aggressively to distinguish themselves, Helsinki and Tallinn willingly rebuilt themselves as conjoined twins.

People who move back and forth frequently refer to "the other side of the lake." Anna is one of those, having traded her apartment in *Vallila*, uptown Helsinki, for a townhouse just inside the walls of medieval Tallinn. Although most days she can and does work from home, Anna looks forward to the opportunity to visit her small factory in *Punavuori*.

Seven minutes by tram and Anna finds herself in the center of Punavuori's lumpy streetscape. The district is now living a new revival as its many courtyards, previously closed and divided between housing cooperatives, have been opened up. In the end it was a citizens' initiative in the neighborhood council that pushed through changes to property law and real estate tax and enabled new uses for the large interior spaces of the blocks. Many of the district's courtyards have been converted into thriving pockets of activity including communal gardens, micro industrial parks, and restaurants.

In the past fifteen years, Helsinki has managed to capitalize on its deep legacy of craft. The hybrid businesses of neighborhoods like Punavuori are recognized as world-leading for their unique blend of technical excellence and pragmatic whimsy.

"Fifteen years ago it would have been almost unthinkable to find a chemical research company, bicycle factory, coffee shop, and school all in the same neighborhood, but now this kind of diversity is what allows Helsinki/Tallinn to punch above its weight."

The city's bet on making better use of the numerous courtyards has paid off by creating new jobs, sure, but also by knitting the city together through the casual necessity of collaboration. Small business in the district's many manufacturing hotspots would be difficult propositions on their own, but form an immense asset when joined up into a flexible network of collaborators.

The building on *Tehtaankatu* ("Factory Street") attracted Anna because its courtyard is renovated into something of an industrial piazza. The large doors that line the court reveal behind them enough talent and tools to manufacture just about anything. It's a beautiful and productive chaos.

Today's mix in the block suits Anna's business better than it did in the past. The addition of an appliance repair shop has allowed her to quickly pull in additional help by hiring their staff during downtimes. This diversity makes sense for her business, and also helps the neighborhood feel more knitted together. The man, who operates the adjacent shop, comes out to offer a friendly "mooooooi" as Anna watches the front of her bicycle factory slowly fold into the ceiling.

"What do you have for me today?"

"The coating I mentioned yesterday is behaving better. Nothing sticks to it!"

"When you can figure out how to apply that to carbon fiber we have a mountain bike waiting to happen."

That a nanochemist and a cycling entrepreneur would have anything to chit chat about at the start of the day, let alone collaborate on, was the gamble that the cities of Helsinki and Tallinn took when they adopted the Joined, Overlapping, & Dense strategy. By encouraging a diversity of endeavors to flourish in proximity to each other, by making this legible and by creating new incentives to encourage collaboration between business, individuals, and the public sector, this strategy continues to pay dividends.

The "lake," née Gulf of Finland, is now a go-to node in global innovation conversations, attracting clients from all over the world who desire the best in bespoke products.

Fifteen years ago it would have been almost unthinkable to find scientific research companies, factories, coffee shops and a school all in the same neighborhood, but now this kind of diversity is what allows Helsinki/Tallinn to punch above its weight.

Walking from the courtyard into the depths of her shop, Anna passes by assembly bays of differing levels of messiness containing bicycles at various states of completion. As the lights dance to life, she looks across the low tables of accessories and other wares that occupy the retail half of her shop, and out through the windows to spot the first people of the morning already on a stroll.

Despite a lucrative offer to move her family and the business to Rio de Janeiro, Anna stays because for her Helsinki/Tallinn is a city of happiness. It's a place where small gestures matter, where connections are made easily, and where the streets are diverse and active.

This is a city where one may feel part of the rushing flows of information, goods, and opinion – but still have time to enjoy a cup of tea and a bit of chatter with a friendly neighbor. ■

Lessons from the Summer Cottage

As we are bombarded by the facts of climate change and Earth Overshoot, the traditions of the simple life at the family mökki challenge us to rethink the patterns of our daily lives, and our relationship with the urban environment.

TEXT AND PHOTOS: HELLA HERNBERG

My relatives spend their summers on a rugged island in the outer archipelago of the Eastern Gulf of Finland. The red wooden summer cottage – *mökki* as we say in Finnish – is tiny, with room for a bed, table, fireplace, a small gas stove and a *sauna*. Mökki, sauna and the lakeside or seaside, is the summer reality for millions of Finns. Valuable holiday time is spent in remote woodland with modest facilities, in family cottages that are often shared between different shoots on the family tree.

This red cottage was built from scrap wood in the 1960's. If something needs to be repaired, or a new mooring needs to be built, the house owner looks underneath the cottage for some spare wood that has been collected from here and there. Fresh fish come from the sea, and blueberries and mushrooms are found in the forest. The fridge runs with electricity from a small solar panel, and each drop of rainwater is carefully collected and put to correct use.

Visiting the island is a privilege and a luxury in itself. Without the burden of too many commodities or comforts it is easy to feel relaxed and happy, and life is crystallized in the elemental. Days are spent eating, reading a book, and perhaps rowing the small boat in search of the right stones for a new sauna stove – smoothness and a fist-size are the prized attributes.

Democritus once said: "The right-minded man is he who is not grieved by what he has not, but enjoys what he has. He is fortunate who is happy with moderate means, unfortunate who is unhappy with great possessions."

At the mökki it is easy to agree. Nordic rural traditions are based on simplicity and necessity. It is not that we deliberately deprive ourselves of modern pleasures to be ecological – but it seems like common sense to do so. *Maalaisjärki*, the Finnish for common sense, even translates literally as "countryside sense."

The urban summer cabin by Verstas Architects in Lauttasaari, Helsinki. Photo: Andreas Meichsner

Washed carpets and mattresses drying on a rod normally used for sorting fishing nets in the archipelago.

Clockwise: Baking bread rolls, watching sunsets and washing dishes outside are some of the modest delights of the typical summer cottage. Counter-clockwise: Verstas Architects' tiny cottage stands in a forest-like recreation park in Lauttasaari, full of similar but older cabins. (Photos top right, middle left: Andreas Meichsner)

What else do you need when there is plenty of time, fresh food, good company, and the diversion of thunderstorms on the horizon – all building blocks of a fulfilled life that you cannot put a price on.

Urban Getaway

Despite all the pleasures that a modest cottage in natural surroundings can offer, there can be one irksome problem: travel distance. Many Finns drive from two to five hours for a regular remote weekend getaway. Helsinki's rush hour starts as early as 2pm on Fridays throughout the warm months as people head for their cottages. Friday is spent traveling and Sunday you have to pack things up. There is not so much time left for being relaxed and such intense private travel does not do any good for our nation's carbon footprint.

Ecologically aware architects, **Jussi** and **Riina Palva** from *Verstas Architects*, have come up with an alternative solution. Their little cabin in the *Lauttasaari* recreational park in Helsinki squeezes the pleasure of being in nature into a package with a minimal carbon footprint.

The Palva family designed their urban getaway as a prototype for a fully functional mini-dwelling, which will be mass-produced by the Finnish manufacturer, *Finnlamelli*. Located about five kilometers from downtown Helsinki, near the rocky seashore, amidst a forest of pines that is full of little cottages, the family may feel removed from their daily life while at walking distance from home.

Jussi Palva describes how their idea was born: "We were first planning a summer house further out from Helsinki. We listed the characteristics of our dream vacation home and realized that, if situated far away, it should be big and fully equipped to serve our needs – instead, the most enjoyable solution for us was a small urban cottage where you can go any time without planning too much in advance."

The couple were inspired by boat design to make the best use of every cubic centimeter of the fourteen square meter cabin.

"In boats floor space isn't that essential. The small space needs to be practical, usable and comfortable. In a boat, furniture is often designed as part of the whole structure, and that inspired us to create a nest-like space where every small item and function has its place."

The family has small children and seems quite content with their tiny holiday house. As Mr. Palva says: "The best thing is that we can always chat with our neighbors and it's very easy to invite friends over."

"The little cabin in the Lauttasaari recreational park in Helsinki squeezes the pleasure of being in nature into a package with a minimal carbon footprint."

The Soul of the Sauna

There are approximately two million saunas in Finland – for a population of a little over five million. The sauna, like life at the summer cottage, provides purification of body and mind, and gives us fresh perspective on our petty daily worries. Conversations and unofficial negotiations flow freely in the sauna steam. Fortunately, the luxury of the sauna is available in urban settings too. Helsinki has many traditional public saunas, which bring together a broad range of people.

For designer **Nene Tsuboi**, and architect **Tuomas Toivonen**, the idea of *Kulttuurisauna* (cultural sauna) was crystallized while sitting on the benches of a public sauna in *Kallio*, Helsinki. Their idea combines various sauna traditions with the social and cultural aspects of public baths in a new way.

Tsuboi and Toivonen are going to realize their project in downtown Helsinki. At the shorefront of *Merihaka*, the 1970's *plattenbau* neighborhood, the sauna will be looking across at the newly developing areas of *Hanasaari* and *Kalasatama*. The couple will also organize construction and run the sauna's cultural program.

As Tuomas Toivonen says: "We were designers, we knew how to build, we wanted to contribute to the city, participate in making Helsinki more interesting and enjoyable, and since no-one else would, we were ready to do it ourselves."

The idea of Kulttuurisauna derives from a vision of the young **Alvar Aalto**, which he conceived in an article in *Keskisuomalainen* newspaper in 1925. Opening in summer 2012, the sauna will be a stage for events, such as workshops, seminars, book launches, small exhibitions, chamber music concerts and discussion forums.

Escape to Basics

Traditions related to the sauna and the mökki bring us back to basics. Simpler living can give time to focus on important basic things in life: family, food, time, health and happiness. Unfortunately trips to the mökki often only offer temporary escape from our urban existence into a romanticized idea of the austerity of our grandparents' times.

"The idea of a simpler and more meaningful life should not just be part of an escapologist's routine, or something we only seek beyond the city walls."

The British philosopher, **Kate Soper**, talks about the growing appetite for "alternative hedonism." The concept identifies widespread motivation for less environmentally destructive practices and green consumption. Her finding is that, in a wide range of contexts, not only in alternative circles, there is a growing disaffection with "consumerist" consumption. In Soper's words, people yearn for "certain forms of human interaction that have been eroded." [1]

The modest traditions that many Finns have learnt from the mökki give a new context to discourse on climate change, degrowth and wellbeing.

The idea of a simpler and more meaningful life should not just be part of an escapologist's routine, or something we only seek beyond the city walls. Why shouldn't the city itself offer us uplifting experiences that leave less need for escapism?

Rethinking the relationship between cities and the countryside can inform a new urbanism where cities are less stressful places, and rural

At the outer archipelago, small pine seedlings and moss survive on the rocky ground. Blueberries are some of the delights – and mosquito-stung feet some of the "hardships" – of being in nature.
Previous page: Illustration of the cultural sauna by Nene Tsuboi.

towns more than just resorts that stay virtually empty outside the holiday seasons. Examples like city farming, food circles or local travel are already changing from niche to norm, and point towards a new understanding of urban life.

Helsinkians are fortunate to have plenty of nature close by – and the resources, information and models to pursue a more sustainable and varied urbanism. Even the most remote and desolate areas of Finland possess qualities that many other places in the world are lacking: a livable climate, peace and quiet, and nature not (yet) threatened by earthquakes or hurricanes.

I have been playing with a thought. Could we turn the nationwide mass migration of people to the forests every summer, into a different appreciation of more immaterial values, on a more permanent and wider scale in everyday life?

Perhaps, in a world facing rapid population growth, the low-density areas and green cities of Finland will soon become places where new communities and lifestyles respecting our finite planet will flourish.

---

1 Soper, Kate; Thomas, Lyn (2006). *Alternative Hedonism: a theory and politics of consumption*. London: Cultures of Consumption.
www.consume.bbk.ac.uk

Also: Jackson, Tim (2009). *Prosperity Without Growth? The transition to a sustainable economy*. London: the Sustainable Development Commission.

A New Horizon

Leaving imminent economic collapse and world disaster behind, a cyclist puts his personal energy resources to the test. Could the increasing human population serve more extensively as a renewable energy resource, and how could local services support such an idea?

TEXT AND PHOTOS: TIMO HYPPÖNEN

"Mankind must colonize space or die out." I had read in the newspaper about **Stephen Hawking**'s prediction of the threats that endanger the future of the human race.[1]

It may sound obscure, but the idea is topical. There is widespread recognition that the world's population, especially in the West, consumes more natural resources than the finite planet Earth is able to reproduce. The world is heading towards unstable times: climate is changing, there's a threat of severe economic collapse, and the food crisis may drive nations into wars.

A similar scenario is actually known to have already been drafted in 1798 by **Thomas Robert Malthus**, and later followed by many other scientists and artists.[2] Such predictions make anyone shiver and it is the kind of future I'd surely want to escape. I just don't see myself booking a space flight anytime in the near future. In fact, I assume most of the nine billion others living on Earth by 2050 (according to a UN medium estimate) will be in the same situation.

So where do we go if not space? Our only option is to pursue a more sustainable lifestyle – before it's too late. The stakes are high since upon failure we might well be facing the disaster that Hawking predicted.

What we should do now is to look at the bright side of the dilemma. While natural resources diminish, human resources multiply. In a sustainable ecosystem, couldn't human energy be used as a renewable resource? If traffic is accountable for 20% of our CO_2 emissions, could we actually cut it down by employing manpower in transportation? What would it mean in practice?

I had the opportunity to test this on a brief

Above: The Helsinki horizon opens up in cold winters when you can cycle on the ice.
Below: The view from the Aulanko watchtower at nearby Hämeenlinna.

Various roadside attractions: a local shop, towing service, concert venue for Finnish "Schlager" and a farm shop with a fresh berry juice bar.

work-related trip. Obviously, cycling is a feasible (although not fully exploited) transport option in urban areas. I considered the amount of commuting that goes on between bigger cities and then took this personal, natural resource of mine and hit the road from Helsinki to *Tampere* – to see how it could work.

The 180 km distance between the two cities is about the length of a daily *Tour de France* stage. However, I didn't race to my destination. Instead I enjoyed an escape in the middle of the week. Before departure, I had worked until 4 p.m. I rode five hours to *Hämeenlinna*, where I stayed overnight, and then another five hours in the morning before my appointment at noon in Tampere. I had time to stop and look around a little.

Although not exactly a space adventure, the trip was brilliant. Exercise, experiment and experience combined. Yet mind relieving, practical and cheap – the normal mantra you hear about cycling.

But then, considering doing the same on daily, or even weekly basis, one could describe it as hours of mind-and-butt-numbing monotonous pedal strokes by the highway alongside boring flatland scenery. This would never be a suitable routine for anyone normal. I mean, what is the maximum time you're willing to devote on the daily commute? Riding 180 km to work is far-fetched. Cycling pros would do it faster and more efficiently, but the distance is still too long for commuting – even by car. But for an escape, such a trip can be a pleasure.

Talking about cycling pros, there are a couple of things we can learn from them: optimum cadence, right fuel, good fit on a proper bike, proper clothes and a little bit of practice. All this is irrelevant in the city environment if you hop on a bike for a short distance, but if you reach out, you will notice the difference.

> *"Interesting surroundings support your momentum and local services may fuel your experience – if they still exist."*

The longer the distance, the more support is needed, both mental and physical. Audio can save you, but don't let it block you away from your surroundings. Small towns and villages, farm sites and lake views may well be inhaled in their purity, free from distractions. Interesting surroundings support your momentum and local services may fuel your experience – if they still exist.

On the way from Helsinki to Tampere there are a few places that can inspire the ride and are worth a visit. The small towns of *Hyvinkää*, *Riihimäki* and *Hämeenlinna* each have something to offer. Lakeside mansions such as *Vanajanlinna* and *Aulanko* are beautiful places for an overnight stay.

Continuing towards Tampere, the sights get a little better. There is less traffic and a couple of farmers' markets with fresh goods that are extremely refreshing. The *Rönnvik* vineyard and the fresh berry juice bar of the *Suttisen Tila* farm will definitely juice up your trip. The *Vehoniemi* motor museum, 25 km from Tampere, is located on a pretty ridge.

While looking at the complete journey, you cannot help but wonder why so many countryside services have vanished under contemporary development. Auto markets and gas station complexes have driven the Finnish countryside into a homogenized highway culture and crippled traditional local businesses. The smaller roads, which are more comfortable for cycling, are lacking services. Old nostalgic gas stations have died and the countryside shop windows have been covered with plywood.

Is there anything we can do to change this course? My experience is that cycling in particular needs these places. And these places would need cyclists. Not only as paying customers, but as people who require better services. Today you will have a hard time finding anything but hamburger stands and "pizza kebabs" on the roads between cities.

Demanding better services brings up another issue: nobody else is going to fix these things for us. It takes our personal human resources to do it. The cliché "think global – act local" has not lost its edge but quite the opposite: the services that support our daily routines are vital.

Local businesses create places that make you want to go out there – places that are worth the visit. Hand made, home made and locally made are the kinds of labor that can never be outsourced.

For the random traveler, as well as the day-to-day commuter, the small things on the street corner, such as coffee houses, shops and services, make a significant difference. They are the cyclist's gas stations and the human-scale oases for tourists hungry for inspiration.

---

1 Helsingin Sanomat, 10 August 2010. Originally in The Guardian, 9 August 2010

2 Malthus' concerns were followed, for example, by **John Ruskin** and the arts and crafts movement at the beginning of the 1900's. The global *Club of Rome* think tank has warned about global warming since 1968. Its book, *Limits to Growth*, raised considerable public attention in 1972. The British economist, **E.F. Schumacher**, drew on Buddhist economics in his 1973 pamphlet, *Small is Beautiful*. Recently, the *degrowth* movement, originating in France, has been at the forefront of the discussion challenging our economic system and its dependency on natural resources.

More Than Money

The Helsinki Time Bank shows the power of sharing skills, services and trust in an alternative economy.

TEXT: HELLA HERNBERG · ILLUSTRATION: SANNA PELICCIONI

When I first heard about the idea of a time bank it brought to mind **Michael Ende**'s children's book, *Momo*, in which gray men steal time from people. In the book, written in the 1970's, gray men force people to do everything more efficiently and make them believe they are saving time. In actual fact, people end up living rushed and unhappy lives without realizing it. Sound surprisingly familiar?

The Helsinki Time Bank works in the opposite way: the bank exists so that people can spend their time on things they enjoy doing and that contribute to the public good. The community was born in fall 2009 when a group of friends in the *Kumpula* neighborhood of Helsinki were contemplating the state of the world and got excited about alternative local economies

that they had seen around the world. In October 2009, the Kumpula local exchange circle was created and it quickly grew into the Helsinki Time Bank (*Stadin Aikapankki* in Finnish), a network that now encompasses the entire city. By fall 2011, the group already had over 1,000 members.

A time bank is a community in which people can exchange services and skills. If you like sewing you can mend other members' clothes and, in exchange, get a massage, a babysitter or help with organizing a party. Based on the Community Exchange System (CES) created in South

Africa, the unit of exchange for services is time. Helsinki Time Bank's currency *tovi* (literally a "while") corresponds to one hour of work. The idea rests on the concept of equality — all work has the same value.

The idea of a time bank challenges modern conceptions about what constitutes a good life and what kind of work is valuable. But how does it fit in with busy urban lives? An active member of the Helsinki Time Bank, **Hanna Koppelomäki**, believes that in the end it is only a matter of how to organize time.

"People have varying levels of wealth but, in terms of time, we're all basically equal. We all have 24 hours, seven days a week available – as long as we realize how to master our own time. Perhaps the value of life is based exactly on how people spend their own time. I personally feel enriched by just doing things I enjoy. With a time bank you can decide how rich you want to be."

Koppelomäki joined the Helsinki Time Bank after reading an article about its activities and, before she knew it, she was one of the group's core members. The time bank has been an important tool in changing her life and it has helped her "arrange time" in new ways. "At first it was more about finding the right attitude that would allow me to use the time bank to navigate the hectic stages of life more easily."

"People have varying levels of wealth but, in terms of time, we're all basically equal. We all have 24 hours, seven days a week available, as long as we realize how to master our own time."

So, what kinds of services are actually offered in a time bank? "You can learn new skills or do things together that you wouldn't want to do alone. I've earned tovis by offering, for example, various neighborly favors and consultancy on all kinds of problems. I've spent most of my tovis on my balcony garden, which I set up in the spring mostly with help from the Time Bank. I've also had some clothes mended, a few haircuts, and some electrical repairs carried out. Each exchange has led to a meeting with a new person — usually at least a short chat — and often the discussions have continued over coffee or tea."

"The knowledge that you can not only receive help but also actively give something back to the community can be very rehabilitating."

In the alternative economy everyone has the opportunity to get the help they need while building trust within the community. One can also owe the Time Bank tovis and repay when one has the energy. According to Koppelomäki, it is actually more difficult to ask for a favor than to provide one: "I try to keep in mind that asking for help makes the other person feel needed — and this can be very meaningful for someone. Many are delighted when I call them about an offer. In terms of the vitality of the community, giving and receiving are equally valuable."

In *Momo* the main character is a little girl that, together with her friends, takes on the gray men. Perhaps these modern day neighborhood time banks are like contemporary "Momos" that are battling society's foolishness and saving people's time for something that truly brings them joy?

Finland already has about 15 regional time banks that have an unofficial network. The

banks operate at a neighborhood level but the dreams and ideas in the background tackle societal issues. Could time banks be used more broadly? Could the reciprocal support system offer new kinds of solutions for increasingly pressing future challenges, such as elderly care?

> "The banks operate at a neighborhood level but the dreams and ideas in the background tackle societal issues."

"Often the elderly, the disabled, various patient groups, youths or immigrants are seen as passive receivers of help. They could be included in this reciprocal activity," Koppelomäki suggests. "Everyone has untapped resources – often those who are not doing well now can have relatively the most to offer. The knowledge that you can not only receive help but also actively give something back to the community can be very rehabilitating. Why would the state and municipalities not apply time banks' principles to their activities?"

↳ www.stadinaikapankki.wordpress.com

The New Life of Things

Community lending services let you try new fantastic things, have fun and share the best stuff. Sharing is the future.

TEXT: HELLA HERNBERG

At the very end of the 1990's, **Markku Jussila** dreamed of a society in which people shared their possessions with others and expensive things were used collectively. Everyone could partake in great new activities without having to invest in mediocre or cheap equipment.

Jussila had bought snow safety equipment for skiing trips in the Alps and Norway – equipment that could be used to save off-piste skiers buried in an avalanche. The gear was rather expensive and exotic for the young man, who had only recently transitioned to working life.

"It was great to own extreme skiers' snow safety gear. That made me a tougher skier, right? I started loaning and renting the equipment to others and I was proud of it. It was a natural way to let everybody know that I owned such specialty gear," Jussila explains.

After a few years Jussila's lending circle had grown and he was already a veteran of community sharing. Meanwhile, the idea of an online tool that could make this easier started to develop.

"In 2006 and 2007, Finland was in the middle of an intense climate change debate and people were discussing how to restrain consumption and the abundance of goods. I was inspired to adapt my own experiences of community sharing into a public online service."

The *Kuinoma* (Like Your Own) service was launched in December 2007. It allows people to lend their possessions easily and safely. The service has been mostly used to share sports

For the amateur winter sports person, Helsinki Reuse Centre can be a treasury. Though it's not like *Kuinoma*, where you have the chance to rent quality equipment from proper enthusiasts.

and camping gear.

Jussila recalls that the idea of community lending was foreign to the public at first: "We didn't have any role models. The service was based purely on my own experiences."

"It's been great to hear how Johnny got to participate in the Off-track Skiing World Championships, taking a loaned sleeping bag with him. Or how Janne and his friends managed to organize an ice-fishing competition after renting an ice drill from Kuinoma."

Coming to the 2010's lending has become a trend. Friends are swapping clothes and new service ideas are born. Many lending-based ideas are related to efforts on climate change, such as the challenge of limiting everything you own to 100 things, enjoying a binge-free Christmas, and the boom in downshifting.

The *Nopsa Fashion Library* is a new lending-based idea that was established in Helsinki in summer 2011. Journalists **Liisa Jokinen** and **Hertta Päivärinta** spotted the Swedish *Lånegarderoben* service, which loans vintage and designer clothes instead of selling them.

"We all have closets full of dresses that we use maybe once a year. They take up too much space. Then there are those who rush out for some impulse shopping when a party's approaching, because it's nice to have something new on for an important occasion. It's become a tradition to organize flea markets and clothes swapping parties at home with friends, and the Fashion Library is an extension of this. Some ideas are based on the Lånegarderoben service, and some practices we developed ourselves," says Liisa Jokinen.

Jokinen and Päivärinta asked their favorite designers to join the service. They also supplemented the collection with vintage treasures that they had lying at the bottom of their closets — as they didn't have the heart to cart them off to the flea market. In addition to party clothes and vintage items, the collection includes a lot of shoes and hats.

The fashion library's message is simple: fashion can be consumed and followed ethically and communally. "In addition to the ecological element, the best parts are the collectivity and that you constantly come up with new ideas," Jokinen says. "It's about trying on dresses together and having fun. Lending lowers the threshold for trying new, nice things."

> *"Nopsa Fashion Library is about trying on dresses together and having fun. It lowers the threshold for trying new things."*

While only a few years ago the climate discussion was characterized by moralizing and guilt, it is now alive with new ideas that help people lower their carbon footprint — or at least their moral burden — while doing something you enjoy.

Markku Jussila says: "When Kuinoma was still new we almost got angry at Finns because they didn't start sharing their stuff immediately. Often we made the mistake of preaching and laying on guilt. Then we noticed that people live their everyday lives pretty much to the fullest all the time. They don't necessarily have the energy to change."

It is best to focus on positive experiences. Things done with the help of loaned equipment are often quite unique. "It's been great to hear how Johnny got to participate in the Off-track Skiing World Championships, taking a loaned sleeping bag with him. Or how Janne and his friends managed to organize an ice-fishing competition after renting an ice drill from Kuinoma," Jussila explains.

"Lending is the future," says Liisa Jokinen. The fashion library's customers have been really glad such a service is finally available.

Perhaps Markku Jussila's vision from years ago will soon be everyday reality. In Finland, where public libraries are abundant, there is a solid foundation for public lending. The *Netcycler* site, established in Finland, has already expanded to Germany and the UK. Meanwhile, *Greenriders* encourages people to carpool. People can borrow valuable works of art for special occasions from the public library on Helsinki's *Rikhardinkatu* street. The Reuse Centre even offers transport bicycles that you can use when you want to move larger, borrowed or recycled items without having to use a car.

Lending services have great potential to bring people joy. Loaning items gets people to try and do new things and helps to improve the world a little while doing so.

"I strongly believe that the best way to develop society is through personal joy," Jussila says.

↳ www.kuinoma.fi
www.facebook.com/pages/vaatelainaamo
www.netcycler.fi
www.greenriders.fi

Nopsa Fashion library's collection of vintage and designer clothes and accessories is open for members to try and test new things every second week. Photos: Veikko Kähkönen

Helsinki Beyond the Economy?

Could Helsinki, as the capital of a traditional Nordic welfare society, be the place to foster values beyond narrow economic goals?

TEXT: PAAVO JÄRVENSIVU · ILLUSTRATIONS: PENT TALVET

Living in Helsinki, we should be grateful for the Finns' reputed lack of marketing skills. I will shortly explain why, but first some background on the issue.

If a city is to be open and free, it must respect the views and practices that are radically different, or virtually unrecognizable, from those of the mainstream. It is not so much about tolerance but readiness to understand. This comprehension comes about through personal and social experience rather than evaluation from the outside.

The dominant way of being in contemporary Western society involves an all-encompassing economic worldview and language. This economization is something most of us are not so fond of – at least outside working life – but find it extraordinarily difficult to escape from.

Today's economic thinking ignores its dependency on natural resources and its long-term cultural implications. To see everything in terms of profit, efficiency, competition, brands and consumption therefore implies a very narrow human existence. It also seduces us to increase the production of goods on a planet that is, in the end, turning out to be very finite. This is why I am here arguing for alternatives – something that could be called cultural diversity.

"That economic growth should not be the most important goal for public policy is still taboo."

Consider a short thought experiment: What would you be left with if you were stripped of the brands you like, of commercial background radio/music/noise, and of the continuous feed of news/mails/games in tiny bursts that keep you simultaneously on the pulse of the world and inside your own little world? Could you still feel easy with your friends and come up with things to do? Continue with your everyday life? Or would you actually feel relieved? The answer depends largely on how deeply dependent you are on such mediating technologies and commercial artifacts.

From the global perspective, Helsinki already exhibits a relatively high degree of various forms of non-economic activity. NGOs, neighborhood time banks, and voluntary networks are some examples. These types of activities are important because they encourage thinking and behavior that stand in opposition to the narrow economic mindset. Their growing popularity means that many people are still able to experience things outside the economic realm, making them more resilient in the face of economic turbulence.

This diversity should not be taken as a given. From the global perspective, it has been nearly driven to extinction. Fortunately, there are communities passionately fighting for it. It is no surprise that many of them are placed in Helsinki.

The capital of a Nordic welfare society, or what is left of it, could be one of the best places to begin the necessary transformations towards a thinking that prioritizes cultural and natural values over economic ones.

The groups fostering alternatives have diverse backgrounds but are united through an attitude that is critical yet joyful. One strong example is the *degrowth* movement, according to which continuous economic growth is neither feasible nor desirable. Gearing up for the current level of economic production has meant taking a loan from the planet by exceeding the renewal rate of natural resources without any intention (or capability) to pay back. Few Finns had heard of degrowth two years ago, but now the term keeps popping up here and there.

Degrowth thinking originates from France,[1] and has gained prominence in many European countries, as well as in Canada, during the last decade. In Britain, professor **Tim Jackson** wrote a very influential book, "Prosperity without Growth," while serving as Economics Commissioner on the UK Sustainable Development Commission.

In Finland the movement consists of researchers, activists, officials, people from

various NGOs, and entrepreneurs among others. They have held numerous workshops and lectures about a managed transition from a growth economy to a sustainable society: designers have experimented with design that is not aimed at selling more products, economists have come up with better measures of welfare than GDP, and the list goes on.

Despite growing general interest, we have yet to see Finnish politicians support the idea in public. That economic growth should not be the most important goal for public policy is still taboo.

The basics of the necessary transition are simple: planetary boundaries need to be taken seriously. Activities should be evaluated in terms of their cultural and ecological, and not only economical, effects.

"The basics of the necessary transition are simple: planetary boundaries need to be taken seriously. Activities should be evaluated in terms of their cultural and ecological, and not only economical, effects."

In the context of urban development, this requires a total overhaul of available funding and other support mechanisms, most of which are now targeted at growth companies with little requirements other than economic reporting. Groupon, Citydeal, and other such companies offering group discounts to consumers that have subscribed to their service, are a prime example. During recent years they have reported huge sales figures, but what is their contribution to

urban life? These companies have essentially persuaded consumers to follow discounts rather than their needs.

An investigative mindset is needed to produce real alternatives. It starts by asking questions, not by giving answers. Traditionally, this approach has been at the core of science and art. In the current mechanisms of urban development, driven largely by construction companies and short-term economic goals, the weight of cultural values has been cut down. In order to foster cultural diversity and to build a sustainable future, critical thinking needs to be revived.

The Finns, even in Helsinki, are still not quite as competent in the production and consumption of marketing – the lifestyle required by a growth economy – as some say we should be. And, in terms of a free and open city, this is our blessing.

Not all of us are brand-natives. The examples of time banks, urban farming and neighborhood communities show a strong desire to interact directly with people, things and nature – rather than through distorted messages crafted only for commercial purposes.

In this sense, the chapters in this book are about Helsinki Beyond the Economy, about a place where the economy fosters culture, not the other way around.

---

1 For example: Latouche, Serge (2007). *Petit traité de la décroissance sereine*. Paris: Mille et une nuits.

Contributors

ANTTI ALAVUOTUNKI plays clarinet in the Vallilan Tango orchestra. He is also an active member of the Vallilan Tango cultural association.

CHARLOTTA BOUCHT is a photographer currently documenting the changing landscapes in Helsinki and Terijoki. Her work consists of reportage, portraits, books and exhibitions. She was awarded the Swedish Cultural Foundation art award in 2011.

STEFAN BREMER is a Helsinki based photographic artist. He is interested in Man and in Mankind. The spectrum in his artistic work reaches from light humorous themes to the dark questions of existence.

BRYAN BOYER is an architect interested in the things that bring rise to buildings and cities, and the things that buildings and cities bring rise to. He currently works at Sitra as a Strategic Design Lead.

JAMES CLAY is a mature student of music and Finnish. He is trying to retire from a long career as a copywriter and communications strategist. After ten years in Helsinki he has an unhealthy obsession with "Finnglish" in print and in song.

ELISSA ERIKSSON is a Helsinki based artist and art teacher, who wants to question the everyday patterns of our behavior with a playful attitude. She finds it fascinating to work in the urban environment since public space is full of unwritten rules.

KATJA HAGELSTAM is a photographer and purveyor of all things interesting and beautiful. She can be usually be found in Helsinki, at her new artspace, LoKal, enthusing over a cup of coffee.

TIMO HYPPÖNEN is a creative designer with a background in the underground. He is one of the founders of a local bicycle company, Pelago.

PAAVO JÄRVENSIVU, D.Sc. (econ.), works as a "conceptual scientist" in Mustarinda – an association of artists and researchers fostering critical thinking on ecology, economy, and aesthetics.

TUOMAS JÄÄSKELÄINEN is a Helsinki based editorial designer and photographer. He is co-author of Helsinki Graffiti, the seminal book about the history of graffiti in Finland.

TUUKKA KAILA is a Helsinki based photographer. His work has been exhibited in group and solo shows in Europe and Asia since 1998. He is a freelance editor at the London based monthly skateboard publication, Kingpin.

ILPO KIISKINEN plays contrabass in the Vallilan Tango orchestra. He is also an active member of the Vallilan Tango cultural association.

HANNA KOIKKALAINEN is a freelance photographer who loves dancing, forests, sauna and cycling in the summer night. She mainly works with portraits and reportages for newspapers and magazines.

HETA KUCHKA is a visual artist born in Helsinki. Her media are drawing, large-scale photography and video. She combines autobiography, reality and fiction, bringing up discussions about identity, media and society with a humoristic touch. Heta started the Punajuuri Blockparty in 2010 with a small group of local friends and strangers.

IDA KUKKAPURO is a writer living and working in Helsinki. She edits Trash Magazine and is a member of the Hapnik collective in Punavuori.

VEIKKO KÄHKÖNEN works as a freelance photographer based in Helsinki and Paris. Veikko is interested in people's warm and genuine encounters.

TOMMI LAITIO is a researcher at Demos Helsinki, an independent think tank focused on sustainable happiness. As a recovering journalist, he loves social experimentation, good language and arts for social change.

CARL SEBASTIAN LINDBERG is a visual artist. He works primarily with the moving image, and his works range from video installations to single channel videos, short films and photography.

MERI LOUEKARI is an architect who coordinates Helsinki City Planning Department's "Urban Pilot" project. She is interested in the temporary urban context and has been coordinator of OpenHouseHelsinki since 2007.

SAC MAGIQUE is an illustrator and an Englishman that calls Helsinki his home. When not at his studio he can be found at his miniature cottage doing a spot of DIY between bouts of serious relaxing.

KATHARINA MOEBUS is a hopeless idealist working to make dreams come true. Currently she works together with different NGOs on several design projects in Laos.

KATARINA MURTO is a translator and editor who loves plants and stories.

OK DO is the peripatetic art/design collective of ANNI PUOLAKKA and JENNA SUTELA. It exercises cultural introspection and intervention through publications, installations and performative projects.

SANNA PELLICCIONI is an illustrator and graphic designer who loves colors and light. Sanna is one of the founders of Helsinki Time Bank. She enjoys bringing people together and raising a new sense of community at the grass-roots level.

JOHANNES ROMPPANEN is a documentary photographer with a focus on the things in-between. He works for international magazines and has an interest in social subjects. Johannes has lately been involved in a project about immigrants in Finland and he currently works on topics related to mentally disabled people.

JOEL ROSENBERG is growing an edible forest garden that should feed him in a few decades. Besides that he works as an environmental artist/activist, teacher and nature guide.

TIMO SANTALA is the director of We Love Helsinki and one of the people behind Restaurant Day.

TUOMAS SARPARANTA is a freelance photographer whose work deals with encounters with people and urban life. Originally from Helsinki, Tuomas is studying documentary photography at the University of Wales.

TUOMAS SIITONEN is a Helsinki based architect and graphic designer. He has collaborated on several publications about graffiti and street art, such as the book Helsinki Graffiti from 1998.

TANI SIMBERG is a photographer who has worked with a variety of themes: from theater, events and portraits to book illustrations. She has exhibited in Rio je Janeiro and Helsinki.

HELI SORJONEN is a photographer and documentary film director who chronicles the performing arts. Over the years she has closely documented the Vallilan Tango orchestra around Finland.

MATTI TANSKANEN is a Helsinki based photographer. He works for several hot magazines and other publications.

PENT TALVET works as an industrial designer in Tallinn. Apart from his day job he makes exhilarating illustrations. He likes sailing and carpentry, and dreams of running a café one day.

NENE TSUBOI is an artist and designer from Japan, based in Helsinki. Her projects often relate to architecture and urbanism, and the making of more interesting and enjoyable places.

HEIDI UUTELA is a Helsinki based freelance photographer who has worked with several designers, musicians and artists. Her main interests are storytelling and creative documentary photography.

VALTTERI VÄKEVÄ is a journalist and copywriter with a skateboarding background. He has worked as editor-in-chief at several Finnish skateboard magazines.

Sources & Inspiration

Selected Bibliography

Borasi, Giovanna & Zardini, Mirko (ed.) (2008). Actions – What You Can Do with the City. Amersfoort: Canadian Centre for Architecture / Uitgeverij SUN.

Bornstein, David (2004). How to Change the World – Social Entrepreneurs and the Power of New Ideas. Oxford University Press.

Castells, Manuel (1996). The Rise of the Network Society. Oxford: Blackwell Publishers.

de Certeau, Michel (1984). The Practice of Everyday Life. Berkeley: University of California Press.

Eaton, Ruth (2001). Ideal Cities – Utopianism and the (Un) Built Environment. Antwerp: Thames and Hudson

Franke, Simon & Verhagen, Evert (ed.) (2005). Creativity and the City – How the Creative Economy is Changing the City. Rotterdam: Nai Publishers.

Fuad-Luke, Alastair (2009). Design Activism. Beautiful Strangeness for a Sustainable World. London: Earthscan.

Hassan, Gerry; Mean, Melissa; Tims, Charlie (ed.)(2007). Dreaming City – Glasgow 2020 and the Power of Mass Imagination. London: Aldgate Press.

Hernberg, Hella (2008). Urban Dream Management – Revitalising Urban Residual Areas through Temporary Uses. Master's thesis, Helsinki University of Technology, Department of Architecture.

Hietala Marjatta; Helminen Martti; Lahtinen Merja (2009). Helsinki - Historic Town Atlas. City of Helsinki Statistical Office.

Honoré, Carl (2004). In Praise of Slowness: How a Worldwide Movement is Challenging the Cult of Speed. New York: Harper Collins Publishers.

Isokangas, Antti; Karvala, Kaappo; Von Reiche, Markus (2000). City on sinun – kuinka uusi kaupunkikulttuuri tuli Helsinkiin. Helsinki: Tammi.

Isomursu, Anne & Jääskeläinen, Tuomas (1998). Helsinki Graffiti. Helsinki: Erikoispaino Oy

Jackson, Tim (2009). Prosperity Without Growth? The transition to a sustainable economy. London: the Sustainable Development Commission

Jouet, Jacques (2000). Poèmes de métro. Paris: P.O.L

Jung, Bertel; Saarinen, Eliel (1918). Ett förslag till stadsplan för "Stor Helsingfors": Pro Helsingfors. Helsinki

Kaskinen, Tuuli; Kuittinen, Ulla; Sadeoja, Saija-Riitta; Talasniemi, Anna (2011). Kausiruokaa herkuttelijoille ja ilmastonystäville. Helsinki: Teos.

Latouche, Serge (2007). Petit traité de la décroissance sereine. Paris: Mille et une nuits.

Latour, Bruno (2008). What is the Style of Matters of Concern? Two Lectures in Empirical Philosophy. Assen: Van Gorcum

Lehtovuori, Panu; Hentilä, Helka-Liisa; Bengs, Christer (2003). Temporary uses. The Forgotten Resource of Urban Planning. Urban Catalysts. Helsinki University of Technology, Centre for Urban and Regional Studies, Series C.

Lindfors, Jukka & Salo, Markku (1988). Nupit kaakkoon – Elmu 10 vuotta. Helsinki: Elävän musiikin yhdistys ry / Kustannusosakeyhtiö City.

McDonough, Tom (ed.) (2004). Guy Debord and the Situationist International. Texts and Documents. Cambridge: MIT Press.

Mäenpää, Pasi (2011). Helsinki takaisin jaloilleen: Askelia toimivampaan kaupunkiin. Helsinki: Gaudeamus.

Oksanen, Kimmo (2006). Makasiinit 1899-2006. Helsinki: Helsingin Sanomat.

Overmeyer, Klaus / Studio Urban Catalyst (ed) (2007). Urban Pioneers – Temporary Uses and Urban Development in Berlin. Berlin: Jovis Verlag.

Puolakka, Anni & Sutela, Jenna (ed) (2012). Museum of the Near Future I. Helsinki: OK Do.

Rantanen, Miska (2000). Lepakkoluola. Helsinki: Wsoy.

Rauramo, Ulla (2004). Ruis. Suomalaisten salainen ase. Jyväskylä: Atena Kustannus Oy.

Raymond, Martin & Sanderson, Chris (ed) (2008). crEATe. Eating, Design and Future Food. Berlin: Gestalten.

Reynols, Richard (2008). On Guerrilla Gardening: A Handbook for Gardening without Boundaries. London: Bloomsbury.

Thackara, John (2005). In the Bubble. Designing in a Complex World. Cambridge: MIT Press.

Victor, Peter (2008). Managing Without Growth - Slower By Design, not Disaster. Northhampton, MA: Edward Elgar Publishing.

Vogelzang, Marije (2010). Eat Love. Food Concepts by Eating Designer Marije Vogelzang. Amsterdam: BIS Publishers.

Internet Sources

www.1234viisi.wordpress.com/
www.all.thepublicschool.org/
www.cca-actions.org/
www.cargocollective.com/urbanblooz
www.citta-slow.com
www.cluestoopenhelsinki.com
www.community-exchange.org/
www.dodo.org
www.doprojects.org
www.en.uuttahelsinkia.fi/
www.facebook.com/pages/vaatelainaamo
www.food-designing.com/
www.greenriders.fi
www.guerrillagardening.org
www.identitysearch.net
www.improveverywhere.com/
www.instructables.org
www.kalasatamanvaliaika.fi
www.kallioliike.org
www.kaupunkiviljely.fi/
www.kuinoma.fi
www.kulttuurisauna.posterous.com/
www.mellunkyla.fi
www.netcycler.fi
www.openhousehelsinki.fi
www.peloton.me
www.popupcity.net
www.punajuuri.org
www.restaurantday.org
www.ruokaosuuskunta.fi/
www.satokartta.net
www.stadinaikapankki.wordpress.com
www.streetartutopia.com/
www.theeconomicsofhappiness.org/
www.unconsumption.tumblr.com/
www.upwithkallio.fi
www.urbandreammanagement.com
www.wdc2012helsinki.fi/en/

Helsinki · Helsingfors

1 Lauttasaari
2 Central Helsinki
3 Suomenlinna
4 Ruskeasuo
5 Haaga
6 Käpylä
7 Lammassaari
8 Kruunuvuorenranta
9 Herttoniemi
10 Itäkeskus
11 Mellunkylä
12 Vuosaari

About the Editor

Hella Hernberg is officially a Finnish architect but finds it hard to describe her work and interests in one word.

Hella's approach to architecture extends beyond buildings. She is fascinated by what's happening next to the planned and built, and how leftover spaces and materials adapt to new uses. She currently runs a workspace shared with other creative minds in an empty harbor warehouse on the rapidly transforming Jätkäsaari dockside – at the epicenter of Helsinki's urban change.
www.hellahernberg.com

Urban Dream Management, founded by Hella Hernberg in 2009, is an design practice and online journal. It focuses on the creative use of urban space and on new, collective approaches to creating more inspiring and sustainable environments.
www.urbandreammanagement.com

Helsinki Beyond Dreams is part of the official program of World Design Capital Helsinki 2012.